The Awesome Books for Awesome People Series by The Angry Whippet

Also available:

More books (
way, stay tu

In no particular order...

1. Two-Face Bilingual

People who can speak more than one language change personality depending on the language they're speaking in.

2. Old School

Harvard University temporarily lost the title of "oldest university in the United States" when the US colonized the Philippines in 1899. Manila's Universidad de Santo Tomas, founded in 1611, predated Harvard by 25 years and was "the oldest university" until 1946, when the Philippines gained its independence.

3. A Moment, Please

In the Middle Ages, a moment was considered an actual measurement of time. The reference to the word "moment" goes back to 1398, when John of Trevisa, a Cornish writer and translator of the time, wrote that there were 40 moments in an hour. A moment in those days was considered to be 90 seconds long.

4. Hard as Nails

The honey badger is widely recognized as the world's most fearless creature.

They feast on porcupines and deadly snakes, attack beehives for honey, steal baby cheetahs, and snatch food from hungry lions. Their mothers also expose them to venom from an early age to build an immunity.

5. Don't Scratch, You'll Make it Worse

They say you shouldn't scratch an itch, and they have a good reason. Skin is the only part of the human body that can feel both pain and an itch.

Scratching an itch causes mild pain, which makes the neurons in the body transfer pain signals to the brain instead of itch signals.

This can cause the brain to release serotonin, a naturally occurring chemical that is used to control pain.

Unfortunately, this chemical can also cause the itching sensation to worsen. The more you scratch, the more serotonin is released, and so the itch continuously comes back worse.

6. Guardians of the Galax-Sea

Humpback whales are known to save other species of animal from killer whale attacks. They have been observed many times protecting animals such as seals and sunfish, putting themselves in harm's way for no apparent reason.

Killer whales, also known as orcas, attack humpbacks when they are young and vulnerable. One theory is that the humpback's rescuing behavior has evolved to help the species through its early stages of life.

Another theory is that the humpbacks are responding to the sounds of orcas as they hunt. Others have speculated the humpback is capable of empathy, and it just wants to help.

7. As cavefish grow older, the eyes they are born with eventually fall off.

8.

People with blue eyes tend to have a higher tolerance to alcohol.

9.

The screaming at Beatles concerts was so loud that no one could hear them play - not even the band themselves.

10.

Cuddling pets and loved ones can reduce the healing time of wounds.

11.

Eating spicy foods can boost metabolism, increasing fat burning up to 16 percent.

12.

According to research, people are two times more likely to die from loneliness than being overweight in later life.

13.

Exercise reorganizes the brain to be more resilient to stress.

14. Saffron Barnet

Ancient Greek king Alexander the Great washed his hair in saffron to keep it a nice shiny orange color. He also believed it helped to heal his wounds after battle.

In his time (356 B.C. – 323 B.C.), saffron was rarer than diamonds and more expensive than gold.

15. Seeing Things in the Dark

If you have ever been in a room with zero light for some time, then you may have noticed that even though it is pitch black, you can make out a dark grey shade.

This is called "eigengrau" (also known as brain gray), and occurs thanks to a process known as isomerization. Normally, isomerization occurs when light stimulates a protein in our eyes known as rhodopsin.

However, this process also occurs spontaneously, and so you are able to see varying shades of gray when in a dark room for an extended period of time.

16. It's a Dog's Life

The world's tallest recorded dog to date is a Great Dane called Freddy, from Norfolk in England. On his hind legs, the pooch stands at a staggering 7ft, or 2.133 meters.

In standard doggy measurements, when the pup is on all fours, he towers high at 3.39ft (1.035 meters).

17. Walking can boost creative thinking up to 60%.

18. The End is (Not Really) Nigh

But it is definitely on its way. Our sun will burn through its supply of hydrogen for around 130 million years, after which it will begin to burn helium.

During this time, the sun will expand, eventually consuming the inner most three planets – Mercury, Venus - and our very own Earth.

19. The dot above the letter "i" is called a tittle.

20. Underwater Elevation

The Earth's longest chain of mountains is underwater. The mid-ocean ridge, as it is known, is almost completely underwater, and stretches across a distance of 37,000 miles (65,000 kilometers).

It is widely believed that this submerged spectacle has been explored less than the surface of Venus or Mars.

21. When the Raiding Stops...

...go skiing. During the Viking age, the fearsome Norsemen regarded skiing as an efficient way to get around, and it was also a popular form of recreation.

The Vikings even worshipped a god of skiing, the supposedly handsome Ullr, who was the stepson of Thor.

22. Say Cheeeeese!

Cheese was discovered accidentally by storing milk in a container lined with an animal's stomach. An enzyme from the stomach caused the milk to separate the whey from the curd (the curd being the cheese).

Amazingly, this was discovered over 4,000 years ago!

23. Short Reign

Louis XIX was the king of France for a whole 20 minutes after his father Charles X abdicated in July 1830. Louis himself then abdicated so that his nephew, the Duke of Bordeaux, could take the crown.

24. Death Did Us Part

It is legal to marry a dead person in France if you can prove the deceased had the intention of marrying you before they died. You must also receive permission from the president.

25. Chocolate Cow

7% of adult Americans believe that chocolate milk comes from brown cows.

While that may seem like a small cut, that's still roughly 15 million people that believe in chocolate cows.

26. As of December 2020, Mount Everest is 33 inches (86 cm) taller than it was in 1954.

27. Battle Tree

In 1917, during World War I, German forces built a 25-foot-tall armor-plated fake tree with a soldier in it to spy on Allied forces.

The Germans waited until nightfall to cut down a real tree to replace it with the fake one, all the while firing artillery so that the British forces wouldn't hear the axes.

28. Baby Songs

Research has shown that pregnant dolphins will sing a signature whistle to their babies while still in the womb.

Baby dolphins will eventually make their own individual whistles, but during the first stages of life, they will use the one they learned in the womb from their mother.

29. Dangerous Driving

The first car to receive a speeding ticket was an 1896 Motor Carriage in Kent, England.

Driver Walter Arnold was pulled over by a police officer who chased him down on a bicycle, and was fined for speeding at 8 mph in a 2 mph zone.

30. A group of hippos is known as a "bloat."

31. Unlucky Jack

Jack Daniel, the founder of the famous whisky Jack Daniels, died after kicking a safe.

He was unlucky enough to suffer an infection in his toe after breaking it on the solid money box, and he eventually succumbed to blood poisoning.

32. Guinea Another One

Guinea pigs are extremely sociable animals. So sociable in fact, that according to the government of Switzerland, owning just one of the little creatures on its own will get you in to trouble.

Anything less than two guinea pigs in one enclosure is considered animal abuse, and is therefore illegal.

33. You ******* ****

On the day of the funeral of the 7th President of the United States, Andrew Jackson's parrot, named Poll, had to be escorted from his former master's funeral.

He was apparently ejected for "swearing so loud and long as to disturb the people and had to be carried from the house."

Exactly what the bird said, or what happened to it after, is unknown.

34. Thumbs Up!

If you hold your thumb up for one second, 100 billion subatomic particles known as neutrinos will pass through your thumbnail.

8.5 minutes ago, those neutrinos were in the heart of the Sun.

35. Pando

A grove of trees in Utah known as Pando (Latin for "I spread") is actually one tree connected by a single and incredibly vast underground organism – it has produced over 47,000 genetically identical stems.

Pando has conquered over 100 acres of land, and while it is incredibly difficult to give it an exact number, it is estimated to be around 80,000 years old.

Sadly, this impressive feat of nature is now in decline, and specialists fear Pando may be entering the last phase of its incredibly long life.

36. Why so serious?

A fear of being happy is known as "cherophobia." The illness, the name of which is derived from the Greek word "chero" – which means to rejoice – is classified as an anxiety disorder.

One characteristic of the condition is a fear of disaster following good fortune - or the balancing of karma.

37. Jupiter's Ring

Although not as obvious as Saturn's, Jupiter actually has its own ring system. It begins 57,100 miles above Jupiter's cloud tops and extends to over 139,800 miles from the planet.

Even though you can't see them, they are between 770 to 5,800 miles thick.

38. Over 1 million Earth's could fit inside the sun.

39. The Sun rotates quicker at its equator. This is known as differential rotation.

40. Moon Mystery

Nobody is certain how the moon formed. One theory is that a Mars-sized rock named Theia crashed into Earth around 4.5 billion years ago. The rock exploded into many smaller rocks in the collision, and they formed together to make our moon.

41. Welcome to the Invisiverse

According to science, only about 4.9% of our universe is actually visible. This percentage is made of what is perceivable to us - the atoms that make up what we can see and touch.

The other 95.1% is a mixture of dark matter and dark energy. Scientists know dark matter exists because it interacts with the gravity of the things we can see, and they estimate it equates to 26.8% of the things we can't see. Dark energy accounts for 68.3%, is invisible, and fills all of space.

42. There are more stars in the whole of the universe than there are grains of sand on all the beaches in the world.

43. The sunset on Mars is blue.

44. Moonruptions

The Lunar Reconnaissance Orbiter (LRO), a NASA spacecraft that arrived at the moon in 2009, found evidence to suggest that within the last 100 million years, there were in fact active volcanoes on the moon.

45. I Used to be a Planet

With a land mass of 6,601,668 square miles, you could theoretically wrap Russia around the ex-planet Pluto, which has 6,427,805 square miles of land mass.

46. The Dark Side of the Moon

During the day on the moon (the sunny side of the moon), the temperature can reach as high as 273 F (134 C).

Conversely, on the dark side of the moon, it can get as cold as –243 F (–153 C).

47. Roman Ruin

The Battle of Cannae was the worst defeat ever inflicted upon Rome.

Hannibal Barca of Carthage led an inferior force of around 50,000 men against the mighty Empire. The Romans, fielding around 80,000 men, suffered casualties and captures totaling around 50,000 to 70,000 men.

To this day, it is still considered to be one of the greatest military victories, as well as one of the most calamitous defeats.

48. Spuds Away

It was widely reported that during the second world war in 1943, the USS O'Bannon engaged a Japanese submarine with nothing but potatoes after realizing they were too close to lower the ship's guns.

However, the ship's Commanding Officer Donald MacDonald, has always denied this account.

"I've been trying to drive a stake through this story for years," he once said.

Despite many people believing the story to this day, it is apparently false.

49. Hat History

Have you ever wondered why chefs wear such tall hats? Officially called a toque, which is Arabic for hat, one tale of its origin dates back to 146 BCE, when the Byzantine Empire invaded Greece.

When the invasion began, Greek chefs fled to monasteries for protection and took to wearing the toques to blend in with the monks. Long after the attackers were pushed back, the chefs continued to wear the hats as a form of rebellion.

The folds, or pleats in the hat, can number up to 100 – the number of ways there are to cook an egg.

50. Silent Giant

Elephant's feet have such soft padding that they can walk around almost completely silently. They also use their giant feet to "listen" to sub-sonic rumbles made by other elephants through vibrations in the ground.

51. Rats!

Rat's whiskers are more sensitive than human fingertips. As the rodents move around, they brush the delicate hairs on everything around them to help build a picture of the environment they are in.

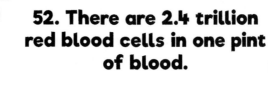

52. There are 2.4 trillion red blood cells in one pint of blood.

53. Eye Spy

The Moken are a tribe of around 2,000 - 3,000 people who live a semi-nomadic lifestyle, and can be found on islands in the Andaman Sea on the west coast of Thailand.

The children can spot small items such as clams beneath the waves with no difficulty. After some studying, scientists discovered that the children of the tribe have learned to constrict their pupils while swimming.

This enables them to have similar vision to dolphins and seals, and they have honed this skill to become efficient hunters.

54. Mon Dieu!

Between the years of 1066 and 1362, French was the official language of England.

After William the Conquerors' occupation of the tiny island, Anglo-Norman French was introduced, and the language was spoken by royalty and people of authority.

Eventually, in 1362, English become the official language after parliament passed the Pleading in English Act, mainly because the commoners of the land had no idea of what was being said in court.

55. It takes more calories to eat a stick of celery than are in it to begin with, making celery a negative calorie food.

56.
Scotland is home to the world's tallest hedge. It is over 1,700 feet long and 100 feet high.

57.
There are more chickens than people in England.

58.
Roald Dahl, the world-famous children's author, was born in Cardiff, Wales, in 1916.

59.
Halloween originated in Ireland as the festival of Samhain, meaning "end of summer".

60.
"Hippopotomonstrosesquippedaliophobia" is a fear of long words.

61. Diamond Pencils

The lead in pencils, which is really graphite, is made of the same thing as diamonds. Both are pure carbon that happen to form at different pressures and temperatures.

Intense heat and pressure form the carbon atoms into crystals making diamond, while less heat and pressure form the carbon into sheets, making graphite.

62. Sorry, what?

Spoken and written words change so much over time that if you could freeze yourself and wake up 500 years from now, you would not be able to read or understand a word of your own language.

63. Sound of Steel

Sound travels over 14 times faster through steel than through air.

64.

Vincent Van Gogh only sold 1 painting in his whole life - and that was to his own brother!

65. Mordhau

Mordhau, also known as Mordstreich (murder-strike), is a German technique of holding a sword with both hands by the blade, and hitting the opponent with the pommel - the blunt end of the sword.

This allowed the swordsman to use the sword as a hammer. The Mordhau was mainly used in armored combat, although it could also be used to surprise an opponent in close quarters.

66. Portu-Pan

The Portuguese were the first Europeans to reach Japan, all the way back in the 16th century.

To this day, some words spoken in the ancient land are influenced by the Portuguese language. Sabato, for example, is Saturday in Japanese, while in Portuguese it is Sabado.

67.
A group of owls is called a parliament.

68.
Information in the human brain travels at 268 miles per hour.

69. Gamer Surgeons

Researchers have found that surgeons who spend at least three hours a week playing video games make about 37% fewer mistakes in laparoscopic surgery.

Additionally, the gaming surgeons also perform the procedure 27% faster than surgeons who do not play video games.

70. Unclucky

In 1995, Egypt, an 18-year-old farmer climbed in to a 60-foot deep well to rescue a chicken that had fallen in.

Unfortunately, the young man got in to difficulty and began to drown. In a desperate bid to help him, the young man's two brothers and sister went in after him to attempt a rescue.

None of them could swim, and sadly they also drowned. Two elderly farmers who saw what happened attempted to help the family members - and they too were overtaken by the undercurrent. All six were later pulled from the well, along with the chicken.

The chicken survived.

71. How mushroom do you need?

In Malheur National Forest, Oregon, there is a giant mushroom that covers 40,112,390 square feet (3,726,562 square meters).

This isn't a mushroom you'd see on the surface. The vast distance is covered by an underground network known as mycelium.

Across the park you can find many types of mushrooms, however they are all part of the same entity.

---

72. Bird Brain

Crows can distinguish humans apart from each other, and it is possible for the birds to hold grudges against people.

On the other hand, they are also capable of gratitude, and have been known to bring humans gifts.

73. Squeaky Squeezy

Mice can flatten their bodies so efficiently that they can squeeze through gaps as small as 6 millimeters. Next time you are writing something, look at the width of the pen you are holding. That's roughly the size we're talking about!

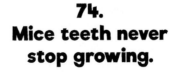

74.
Mice teeth never stop growing.

75. It Be Dark Below!

Pirates really did wear eye patches, but normally not because they were missing an eye.

In fact, they covered one up, so when they went below decks, they had an eye already adjusted to the dark depths of the ship after being out in the bright sunlight above.

76. Ladies of the Seas

While the majority of pirates were men, there were also several notorious women pirates.

Jeanne de Clisson of France (1300 – 1359), a former noblewoman, turned to piracy to avenge her fallen husband after he was executed by the French king for treason. She often targeted French ships in the English Channel, slaughtering the crew, but usually spared one to carry messages to the king.

Mary Read of England (1685 – 1721), was on board a ship that was attacked by pirates, who she then willingly joined. She later joined John "Calico Jack" Rackham, and his companion Anne Bonny of Ireland, another famous female pirate.

The women's careers were successful but short, and all three were eventually arrested. Rackham was executed immediately, but the other two women claimed to be pregnant and received delayed sentences. Read died of fever in 1721.

There is no record of Anne Bonny's fate.

77. Honey Bee Good

Honey does not go bad. In fact, it is recognized as the only food that doesn't spoil.

Over time, it will however crystalize, but this can be solved by simply removing the lid to a honey pot and placing it in warm water.

78. Flyby

The average lifespan of a housefly is around 30 days. In that time, the fly can lay up to 500 eggs, usually in batches of around 100 - 150.

79. Pop's Icicle

At the age of 11, Frank Epperson accidentally invented ice pops by leaving sugary soda powder and water outside on a frosty night. The next morning, he picked up the now frozen treat and licked it clean off of the wooden stirrer he'd left in the mix. He called it the Epsicle - a play on the word's icicle and his name.

Epperson began selling the ice pops around his neighborhood, and many years later, as a grown man, he began selling his creation at a nearby amusement park called Neptune Beach. After incredible success, he applied for a patent in 1924. Eventually, Epperson's children convinced him to change the ice pop's name to Popsicle.

80. An ostrich's eye is bigger than its brain.

81.
Men see fewer shades of color than women, as they have fewer retinal cores in their eyes.

82.
Men's faces maintain a youthful appearance for longer because a man's skin loses its concentration of collagen much slower, making it more resistant to wrinkling.

83.
A man's skin is, on average, 25% thicker than a woman's.

84.
Men can stay warm easier because they have, on average, a higher muscle mass than women. This results in a lower resting body temperature.

85.
During exercise, a man's primary fuel is carbohydrates. For women, it is fat.

86.
Women tend to be able to remember people's faces better than men due to their subconscious analyzing of facial features.

87.
Women have stronger immune systems, possibly due to the ability to give birth.

88.
Due to the different amount of hormones between men and women, on average, women are 14% more likely to survive a serious injury.

89.
Women's muscles are more flexible than men's as they have more elastin, and their lower spine has evolved to accommodate childbirth.

90.
Women have better muscle endurance than men, and on average, can exercise 75% longer.

91.
The longest word you can type from the top row of a keyboard is "typewriter".

92.
Banging your head against a wall burns 150 calories an hour.

93.
Stilts were invented by French shepherds, who needed a way to get around in wet marshes.

94.
The can opener was invented 48 years after the can.

95.
There are 92 nuclear bombs lost at sea.

96.
There are around 365 different languages spoken in Indonesia.

Grass lawns greatly improve air quality around the home and garden. They do this by trapping airborne dust particles and other contaminants around them. Not only that, but a 2,500 square foot lawn can produce enough oxygen for a family of four.

98. Ocean Atlas

Submerged off of the coast of Nassau, the capital of the Bahamas, is an underwater statue known as Ocean Atlas. It is the largest underwater sculpture in the world, reaching up 16 feet (5 meters) from the sea floor, and weighs over 60 tons.

The artwork is a depiction of a local Bohemian girl carrying the weight of the ocean on her shoulders, a reference to the Ancient Greek myth of Atlas, the famous titan condemned to hold up the heavens for all of eternity.

99. Going Your Own Way

Ever noticed an unofficial path leading from one place to another? This is known as a desire path, also known as a game trail, social trail, herd path, fisherman trail, elephant path and bootleg trail, among other names.

It is a path created by erosion by human or animal foot traffic and often represents the shortest or easiest route between two destinations.

100. Young Gyrle

The word "girl" as we know it today originated from the word "gyrle." In the 1300s, "gyrle" was used to describe any child or young person, whether they were a girl or not.

---

101. Turtle Age

Marine turtles have been around for over 100 million years, and even lived alongside the dinosaurs. There are seven species of marine turtle – Hawksbill, Loggerhead, Leatherback, Olive Ridley, Green, Flatback and Kemp's Ridley.

Six of these are at risk of extinction, and there is not enough information about the flatback to know how at risk they are.

---

102. Failed Negotiation

When professional soccer player Giuseppe "Billy" Reina signed a contract to play for Arminia Bielefeld, he requested a clause in his contract stating the club had to build a new house for him for every year he spent with them.

Unfortunately, the German failed to specify the size or type of house, and ended up being the recipient of model houses made of Lego.

103. Golden Flake

In 2008, a cornflake shaped like Illinois sold on eBay for $1350. The auction site initially took down the listing as it violated the company's food policies. On the second attempt, the two sisters selling the flake sold a redemption coupon instead, and cashed in a tidy profit.

104.
"Pteronophobia" is the fear of being tickled by feathers.

105. Ancestral Ailment

About 8 percent of human DNA comes from viruses inserted into our genomes in the distant past, and in many cases into the genomes of our pre-human ancestors millions of years ago.

106. Head for Heights

Scientists have discovered that it is possible for bees to fly higher than Mount Everest. After collecting bees from China's Sichuan Province, the researchers placed the bees in a glass flight chamber, and used a hand pump to slowly pull the air out of it to simulate the conditions the bees would face at higher altitudes.

The bees adapted to the thin air not by beating their wings faster, but by swinging their wings through a wider arc.

One scientist noted how the bees brought their wings closer up towards their nose, and then farther back towards their abdomen.

107. No Show

In 2009, Stephen Hawking held a party for time travelers. He didn't make any mention of it until after the event, so that only those that could travel through time would be able to attend.

Nobody turned up.

108. The act of rushing to clean before a guest arrives is known as "scurryfunge."

109. I'll Follow You

Scientists believe baby turtles can communicate with each other before they hatch, in order to emerge from their eggs at the same time.

A study of Australia's Murray short-necked turtle found the embryos synchronized their hatching to prevent smaller turtles emerging alone and being attacked by predators such as lizards and foxes.

110. Spinosaurus

The biggest predator that ever lived on land was the Spinosaurus, a 56-foot (17m) long fish-eating dinosaur.

Spinosaurus's size was enhanced by its long spines extending up from the backbone, which created a tall arching crest, or something akin to a sail.

111. Shrimp System

A shrimp's heart is located at the bottom of its head. Shrimps also have an open circulatory system, meaning they have no arteries at all, and their organs float directly in blood.

112. More tornados occur in the United Kingdom per square mile than any other country in the world.

113.
There are over **60** different species of eagle.

114.
Eagles can reach as high as **15,000** feet. They tend to fly in long glides in order to conserve energy.

115.
Eagles have a body temperature of **106 F (41 C)** compared to humans that average around **98 F (37 C)**.

116.
The harpy eagle and the Philippine eagle are two of the largest types of eagle, and can have a wingspan of **8 feet** long.

117.
Even though the eagle is the national bird of the United States, there are only two species of sixty worldwide that call North America their home - the bald eagle and the golden eagle.

118.
For every second it exists, a large hurricane releases the energy of 10 atomic bombs.

119. Gravitational Anomaly

Gravity is not the same across various parts of the planet, as Earth is not an exact sphere and is ever so slightly oval in shape.

The poles of the planet are flatter and so the equator bulges slightly. The effect of this is a gravitational change because of the location and elevation of the Earth.

One example of this effect is in the Hudson Bay area of Canada, where objects weigh 1/10 of an ounce less than they should do. There are several proposed theories as to why this occurs, however, it is still a disputed topic.

120. Spam Spam Spam

The term "spam" that is used to refer to junk email originates from a 1970s Monty Python sketch. The sketch featured a group of Vikings belting "spam, spam, spam" to drown out other people who were trying to talk.

The term applies because spam is seen to drown out normal discourse online, much the same as the Vikings in the sketch drowned out the voices of people trying to have a normal conversation.

121. In the next 60 seconds, 101 people will die and 261 babies will be born.

122. Blue Beast

Blue whales are the largest animals ever known to have lived on Earth. These magnificent beasts can be up to 100 feet long, and weigh between 110,000 – 330,000 lbs (50,000 – 150,000 kg).

According to one study, a single mouthful of food swallowed by a blue whale can contain 457,000 calories, which is 240 times as much energy as they burn when grabbing that mouthful.

123. Mallard Malefactor

There are many unusual laws across the world today. One of the more bizarre ones comes from Florida, USA, where it is illegal to walk across the Wisconsin border with a duck on your head.

124. Happy Birthdays!

South Koreans have two different ages. They have their international age, which is the number of years since they were born, and their Korean age, which can be one or two years higher.

This is because babies are considered to be a year old the day they are born. South Korea is the only nation in East Asia to still use this traditional system, however, lawmakers are looking to bring it to an end as soon as possible.

**125.
At the height of its power in 400 B.C., the Greek city of Sparta had 25,000 citizens and 500,000 slaves.**

126. Handy Latin

It is speculated that Italian hand gestures were originally formed to communicate with people that spoke a different dialect.

Although Italian is the official language of Italy, the country actually has some 34 spoken languages and related dialects. Most of these languages are Romance-based, meaning that they evolved from Vulgar Latin. These include Sicilian, Neapolitan and Sardinian, amongst others.

Until around the 60s and 70s, most of the people in Italy only spoke in their local dialect. Because of this, people from different regions started communicating using their hands together with words in order to be understood. Hand gestures spread all across the country and eventually became a big part of communication in Italy.

127.
A duck is called a duck because it ducks its head under the water to feed.

128. Neigh Way

Spiral staircases were installed in fire stations in the 1800s to stop the horses that pulled the engines going up the stairs when they smelled food cooking.

129. No Rush

During the 1908 Olympics in London, the Russians showed up 12 days late because they were using the Julian calendar instead of the Gregorian calendar.

130. Who is This Man?

People who experience auditory hallucinations will almost always hear a male voice. Psychiatrists believe the reason behind this could be explained by the fact that the female voice is so much more complex, and the brain finds it much harder to create a false female voice accurately.

131. Sad Goat Noises

The word "tragedy" originates from the English word "tragedie", which itself can be traced back to the Latin word "tragoedia."

Tragoedia comes from the Greek word "tragōidía", which means "goat song."

It is believed that Greek tragedies were known as goat songs because the prize in Athenian play competitions was a live goat.

132. So you're saying there's a chance?

There are roughly 8 * (10^67) different possible card combinations in a standard 52-card deck – that's an 8 followed by 67 zeros.

This means there are more card combinations than there are atoms in the observable universe. Nobody has ever, or likely will, hold the same combination of cards as you have while playing a game.

133. Poker Face

Today, sunglasses are used as a fashion accessory, or to prevent harmful sun rays from slowly damaging our eyes.

However, in 12th century China, sunglasses cut from smoky quartz were used to hide the facial expressions of judges when questioning witnesses, as they didn't want to give away what they were thinking.

---

134. Unnaturally Orange

Oranges are not a naturally occurring fruit and are actually a hybrid of pomelos and tangerines. They were first cultivated in Southeast Asia and are green when they begin life. To help them become the color we know, they are exposed to ethylene gas.

Their name derives from the Arabic word "nāranj", which was later adopted in to the English language as "narange" in the 14th century.

As time went by, the "n" gradually faded out of use in a process known as wrong word division, which incidentally gave us words like newt (originally "ewt") and ingot (originally "lingot").

**135.
Lobsters taste
with their feet.**

136.
Frigatebirds can sleep while flying, averaging about 42 minutes per day.

137. Secret Squid

The Hawaiian bobtail squid can hide its own shadow because of bacteria in its gut known as Vibrio fischeri. Through a combination of light detectors on its back and the bioluminescent bacteria in its gut, it can perfectly match the brightness of the moon and stars above the water.

138. Because of the increasing temperatures in the summer months, Paris's Eiffel Tower can grow by up to 6 inches.

139. Nuclear Moon

In 1958, the United States Air Force reportedly thought it was a good idea to detonate a nuclear bomb on the surface of the moon.

The top-secret project, known as "A Study of Lunar Research Flights," also called Project A119, was seemingly born out of a desire to intimidate the Soviet Union after it had launched Sputnik I.

140. Med Mega Flood

It is theorized that the largest flood in Earth's history created the Mediterranean.

Named after the geologic age it occurred in (from 5.3 to 3.6 million years ago) – The Zanclean flood, also known as the Zanclean deluge, is thought to be the largest flood ever. Studies conducted in 2009 showed water violently rushed into the then dry Mediterranean, after shifting tectonic plates reopened the Strait of Gibraltar.

141. Not Born to Be Wild

There are no such thing as wild alpacas. Alpacas are actually a domesticated version of the vicuña, which are also related to llamas.

142. Spicy Bang

Indian military scientists have developed a chili grenade for use by the Indian Armed Forces. The grenades use bhut jolokia, aka the ghost pepper, which is one of the world's spiciest chili peppers.

The weapon emits an incredibly powerful skin and eye irritant, as well as an extremely strong smell that causes those that come in to contact to leave their cover or become physically incapacitated by the grenade's load.

143. There are more twins being born now than ever before.

144. Small Profit

When Apple was buying rural land to build its North Carolina data center, one family refused to sell a 1-acre plot they had purchased for $6,000. After rejecting every offer, Apple told them to name a price.

They sold the plot for $1.7 million.

145. Now Listen Ear

Studies have shown that our left and right ears each respond differently to certain sounds. The right ear responds more to speech, while the left ear is more tuned in to music, emotion, and intuition.

Researchers believe this is because speech is processed primarily in the left hemisphere of the brain, while music is processed in the right hemisphere.

146. Armordillo

Much to the delight of comedian Ricky Gervias, who tweeted "Karmadillo" at the news, a man from Texas learned his own fascinating fact when a bullet he fired at an armadillo ricocheted and hit him square in the jaw.

The gunman was treated for a minor injury, and the armadillo apparently wondered off unscathed.

Another man in Georgia also learned this lesson when a bullet he fired at one of the little creatures bounced off the animal's armor, hit a fence, went through the door of his mother's mobile home, and then hit her in the back.

147.
Your heart beats around 100,000 times a day.

148.
It is illegal for frogs to croak after 11 PM in Memphis, Tennessee.

149.
Scotland's national animal is a unicorn.

150.
Candy floss, or cotton candy, was invented by a dentist.

151.
The word for the phobia of words spelled backwards is, coincidently, Aidohphobia.

152.
Over 80 percent of body fat leaves the body through exhaling, making the lungs the primary organ through which we lose weight.

153.
Sonic the Hedgehog's middle name is Maurice.

154.
The average cumulus cloud weighs 500 tons (500,000 kg.)

155.
Highway 401 in Ontario, Canada, is North America's busiest highway, with some days exceeding half a million cars worth of traffic.

156.
Having red hair and blue eyes is the rarest color combination possible. The odds of having both traits are around 0.17%.

157.
Oxford University is 200 years older than the Aztecs, 300 years older than Machu Picchu, and 150 years older than the Easter Island heads.

158. Blind Bet

On 20th October 1986, onboard the Soviet domestic passenger flight Aeroflot Flight 6502, pilot in command Alexander Kliuyev made a bet with his co-pilot Gennady Zhirnov that he could land the plane with the cockpit curtains closed.

Ignoring the ground proximity warnings at 203 feet, the aircraft eventually touched down at a speed of 150 knots (98 mph) and flipped upside down before bursting in to flames.

Sixty-three people were killed during the accident, and a further 7 died in hospital from their injuries.

Zhirnov made no attempt to avoid the crash but tried to save the passengers after. He died of a cardiac arrest on the way to hospital.

Kliuyev was prosecuted and sentenced to 15 years in prison, though this was later reduced to 6.

159. Immortal Blob

Turritopsis dohrnii, a jellyfish discovered in the Mediterranean in 1883, was found to have an incredibly unique ability when studied in the 1990s.

When facing starvation, physical damage or other potentially life-threatening situations, the creature transforms all of its existing cells into a younger state.

The jellyfish turns itself into a blob-like cyst, which develops into a polyp colony - the first stages of life in a jellyfish. Muscle cells become nerve cells and can even go as far as transforming in to sperm or eggs.

Turritopsis is able to reproduce by itself, resulting in the polyp colony spawning hundreds of genetically identical jellyfish.

160. Queen of Tragedy

Lady Jane Grey is remembered in British history as the monarch with the shortest reign.

After the death of her cousin King Edward VI on 6th July 1553, she was proclaimed Queen of England even though she was only fifth in line. Edward, being a protestant, had personally chosen Lady Jane to ascend to the throne as she shared his faith. He knew that if the throne were to go to the first in line, his half-sister Mary and daughter of Henry VIII, she would take England back in to the Catholic faith.

Lady Jane was said to be beautiful and intelligent. She was fluent in French and Italian, and studied Latin, Greek and Hebrew. None of these traits would help her with the troubles to come.

It wasn't long before the country rose in favor of the direct and true royal line. Lady Jane was eventually deposed, and the Council declared Mary the Queen of England.

Unfortunately, Lady Jane's father was Sir Thomas Wyatt, an English soldier turned rebel. Wyatt was involved in a conspiracy against the marriage of Mary to Phillip of Spain, and raised an army of Kentish men before marching on London. He was captured and beheaded.

After the rebellion was quashed, Lady Jane and her husband, Lord Guildford Dudley, were sentenced to death.

Guildford was executed first on Tower Hill, and his body was removed by horse and cart. Lady Jane herself was then taken to the block.

It is said she died bravely, asking the executioner to "please dispatch me quickly." She tied her kerchief around her eyes, laid her head upon the block, and stretched out her arms before saying "Lord, into thy hands I commit my soul."

Lady Jane's reign lasted for just nine days, 10th to 19th July 1553.

161. Boing!

The bouncy ball was patented in 1966 by a Californian chemist named Norman Stingley. In 1965, Stingley spent his spare time experimenting with rubber. He compressed various scraps of synthetic rubber together under about 3,500 pounds per square inch of pressure. The result was a compressed rubber ball with an extreme resilience and high bounce.

162. Time Flies

1.4 billion years ago, when the moon was a bit closer and Earth's rotation was faster, a full day lasted just over 18 hours. 3.5 billion years ago, a day only lasted for 12 hours. Because the moon is constantly and ever so slightly moving away from us over time, 0.00001542857 seconds are added to every year.

163. Bless You!

You may have noticed that dogs tend to sneeze when they are playing. This is known as play sneezing and simply means that the dog is having fun!

164. An estimated 3 million shipwrecks are spread across ocean floors around the planet.

165. Buried Alive

Scientists today believe that Alexander the Great suffered from a very rare neurological disorder now known as Guillain-Barré Syndrome, a condition that can cause whole body paralysis.

After 12 days of agony, Alexander finally "passed away" from his illness – or so it seemed. His body did not decompose for some days after his "death" – suggesting that Alexander was not dead, but paralyzed, and was fully aware of what was going on around him as he was buried alive.

166. Koala Bean

A baby koala when born is roughly 20 millimeters long, less than 1 gram in weight, and looks like a pink jelly bean.

167. Outnumbered 10 to 1

The human body is made up of around ten trillion different cells, but is home to one hundred trillion bacterial ones. This is known as a microbiome, and impacts everything from health to digestion.

168. Pocket Money

In Japan, married women control the purse strings. Three quarters of Japanese men hand their entire salary over to their wives every month, and in return they receive "okozukai", which translates to pocket money.

169. Sunshine is a natural antidepressant.

170.
It's not something that comes up often as hedgehogs are solitary creatures, but a group of them together is called an "array."

171.
A hedgehog has somewhere between 5,000 and 7,000 spines on their back.

172.
Hedgehogs are largely immune to snake venom, and one hedgehog in particular, the long-eared Hedgehog, is even capable of killing vipers.

173.
There are 17 different species of hedgehog. Types of hog include the Amur, the Four-toed, the Bare-Bellied and the Gaoligong hedgehog.

174.
One hedgehog can be carrying anything up to 500 fleas at a time, however the type of flea, known as Archaepsylla erinacei, rarely bites humans.

175. Yellin' Yeltsin

In 1994, former Russian president Boris Yeltsin got drunk during a White House visit and wandered into the streets of Washington. Secret Service agents found him yelling for a taxi in his underwear.

He wanted some nighttime pizza.

176. Reverse Temperatures

There exists in the ocean a certain type of plankton known as dinoflagellates. These microscopic creatures are responsible for harmful algal blooms, a name given for rapid overgrowths of algae in water.

Dinoflagellates can produce extremely potent toxins. Should an individual be unfortunate enough to eat seafood contaminated by these toxins, the feeling of hot and cold is reversed within the body, and the sufferer will also experience hallucinations. These symptoms can last a few weeks, or if you're very unlucky, for several years.

177. Carry Me, Darling

Finland is host to an annual wife carrying competition. Known locally as "eukonkanto," husbands from all over the world carry their wives in a 253.5 meter race (about 831 feet) involving two land obstacles and a one meter (3.2 feet) deep water obstacle.

The wife must weigh at least 108 lbs, lest she be burdened with additional weight. Official rules also state that contestants must enjoy themselves. Special prizes are awarded for the most entertaining couple, best costume and the strongest carrier.

178.
Switzerland has over 1,500 lakes.

179.
Switzerland is home to the world's longest staircase, with a step count of 11,674 and a height of 5,470 feet (1,667 meters).

180.
Less than 15% of the Alps are actually Swiss.

181.
The country has four national languages - French, German, Italian and Romansh.

182.
Switzerland is approximately 15,937 sq miles, barely one tenth the size of California.

183.
There is a psychological disorder known as boanthropy, in which the sufferer believes they are a cow.

184.
An impending tornado can turn the sky green.

185.
The Facebook logo is blue because Mark Zuckerberg has red-green color blindness.

186.
The density of pain receptors in the cornea is 300-600 times greater than skin.

187.
There are only three countries in the entire world that don't use the metric system - Liberia, Myanmar, and the United States.

188. Tricky Toddler

Researchers from the University of Toronto found that children who are good liars are more likely to have future social success.

If you find yourself being fooled by a 2-year-old, you're potentially standing in front of a very smart kid.

189. The Snake Pit

There is an island off the coast of Brazil called Ilha da Queimada Grande, and it is considered to be one of the most dangerous islands in the world.

It is estimated that 2,000 to 4,000 golden lancehead vipers – one of the deadliest snakes in the world - live on the island. Estimates are that there is one snake for every 10 square feet (1 square meter) in some spots.

People have claimed in the past that the snakes were put there by pirates wanting to protect their buried treasures, but the more likely explanation is that the snakes evolved on the island over thousands of years, completely untouched by human intervention.

When sea levels rose over 10,000 years ago, Ilha da Queimada Grande was separated from the Brazilian mainland. As a result, the snakes were left with no ground level predators, but they also had no ground level prey. Over the years, this caused the snakes there to evolve differently.

Their only option for food came from the skies, but as the snakes have no way of tracking prey through the air, they evolved incredibly potent venom capable of incapacitating almost anything immediately.

190. Bubblegum Broccoli

Fast-food giant McDonalds once developed bubblegum flavored broccoli in an attempt to provide healthier food options for children. When tested on their target audience, it unsurprisingly didn't go too well, causing nothing more than a lot of confusion.

191. Tree of Pain

An endangered species of tree known as the manchineel tree produces a fruit so dangerous it has earned the name "manzanita de la muerte," or little apple of death.

It resembles a small green crabapple and is about 1 to 2 inches wide. The fruit, if eaten, can cause hours of agony and even death with a single bite.

In fact, the fruit is so potent that if anyone were to stand underneath one during rainfall, any water landing on the skin can cause blisters.

192. Criminal Cheese

There is a type of Sardinian cheese known as Casu Marzu, and it is highly illegal. Translated in to English, it means "rotten cheese."

It is a traditional sheep's milk cheese that is intentionally left outside so that female Piophila casei cheese flies can lay their 500 or more eggs in it. Once the eggs hatch and the larvae eat through the cheese, the acid from the maggot's digestive system breaks down the fat, making the cheese very soft.

Only when the maggots have died is the cheese considered to be unsafe by Sardinian cheese connoisseurs, otherwise it is perfectly fine to eat, wriggling maggots and all.

193. Happy & Healthy

Being grateful reduces the chance you will feel aches and pains, improves psychological health, helps you sleep better and reduces aggression.

194. Tilted Tower

Italy's Leaning Tower of Pisa didn't lean over time. It was never straight and began to tilt when construction on the third floor started. Building of the Tower was suspended for many years, and when it eventually resumed, the remaining floors were built with a curvature opposite to the tilt.

195. Larger Than Life

The tallest married couple ever recorded was Canadian Anna Haining Swan (1846 – 1888) who measured in at 7 ft 11 in, and American Martin Van Buren Bates (1837 – 1919) who was slightly shorter at 7 ft 9 in. The two met on an Atlantic Crossing and were married in London on 17th June 1871. When Anna eventually gave birth, the baby weighed 22 pounds!

196. Tortured Millers

Treadmills today are used to help us exercise, but back in 1818, they were first used as a form of punishment.

The treadmill, or "everlasting staircase," was invented by British engineer Sir William Cubitt as a way of usefully employing convicted criminals. The devices were wide enough to handle about 40 people at the same time and were commonly used to grind corn or pump water, although some had no purpose at all and were simply a form of torture.

Using treadmills for torture was eventually abolished in Britain under the Prisons Act of 1898.

197. Mystery Moth

In 1862, someone sent Charles Darwin a flower from Madagascar that had an extremely deep crevasse where the nectar was located. He predicted that there was a moth with an extraordinarily long tongue to reach the nectar.

Xanthopan morganii was discovered nearly 150 years later feeding on the flower.

198. African Samurai

The first non-Japanese samurai, known as Yasuke, arrived in Japan in 1581. He was a 16th century African slave who won the favor of feudal Japan's most powerful warlord at the time - Oda Nobunaga.

Oda had never seen an African before. Like the locals in Japan's then-capital of Kyoto, he was awestruck by Yasuke's height, build, and skin tone.

Yasuke was tall and had military experience. He trained militiamen and, while doing so, he learned various new skills himself, including sword skills and martial arts.

Records of Yasuke became scarcer after Oda took his own life to preserve his honor after suffering defeat to one of his own generals.

Legend has it that Oda's last order to Yasuke was to take his sword and decapitated head to his son in a bid for the clan to keep power.

According to one professor, Yasuke was eventually captured by Oda's enemies but later released because he was not Japanese. He then became a "ronin" - a samurai without a master.

199. Tragic Waste

It is estimated that around 93,000 liters (24,568 gallons) of beer are lost in facial hair every year, and that's just in the UK.

200. Low Pop

During the Stone Age, there were extended periods of time where there were fewer than 1,500 people living in Central Europe.

201. Canine Cruiser

A bulldog named Otto from Lima, Peru, holds the world record for the longest human tunnel traveled by a skateboarding dog after he successfully boarded his way through the legs of 30 people.

202. Moo Shoe

During prohibition in the United States, moonshiners would wear shoes that left hoofprints instead of footprints, helping smugglers and distillers avoid unwanted attention from the authorities.

203. Bottle Bank

In a part of Siberia, Russia, teachers were once paid with vodka. During the month of September in 1998, local authorities did not have enough money to meet the wage bill.

Some 8,000 teachers were originally offered vegetables, toilet paper and funeral accessories but eventually settled for 15 bottles of vodka each.

204. Great Veil

A wedding in Cyprus on 14th August 2018 saw bride Maria Paraskeva wear the longest ever veil. The garment measured in at an impressive 22,841 feet (6,962.6 meters).

---

205. Lottery Hacker

A Michigan mathematician named Jerry Selbee calculated his way to a fortune using the State Lottery.

The operators of the lottery foolishly listed the odds of winning that were associated with each combination of numbers, be it three, four or five matches.

If nobody won the lottery for a particular week, the prize was carried over to the next. After six weeks, or when the jackpot hit the $5 million cap, a "Roll Down" would occur, where the winnings were spread downwards towards lower tiers.

Using a complex mathematical formula, Jerry worked out that it was at this point where the tickets became worth more than their $1 asking price.

Starting with small stakes and small gains, he and his wife were splitting up in to two cars and visiting countless stores across the state, eventually spending hundreds of thousands of dollars for a single Roll Down.

Sometime later, a group of students at MIT also discovered the flaw and started buying tickets.

The story eventually broke in to the news and the lottery was shut down, but Jerry didn't mind – he and his wife had already won $26 million over an entire decade of buying tickets.

206.
"Philophobia" is a fear of falling in love.

207.
The rhyme Humpty Dumpty never mentions that he is an egg.

208.
The letter "X" was first used to represent a kiss in 1763.

209.
63 million pairs of chopsticks are manufactured in China every year.

210.
If a Polar Bear and a Grizzly Bear mate, their offspring is known as a Pizzly Bear.

211.
In order for bread to become toast, it goes through a process known as the Maillard Reaction.

212.
Four times more people speak English as a second language than as a native one.

213.
Fear of the number 13 is known as "triskaidekaphobia."

214.
The hashtag symbol is also called an octothorpe.

215.
In 1893, New Zealand became the first country in the world to give women the right to vote.

216.
Queen Elizabeth II is a trained mechanic.

217.
The act of hoarding books and not reading them is known as "Tsundoku."

218. Independent Extremities

Two-thirds of the neurons in an octopus are located in the creature's tentacles.

Amazingly, these tentacles are able to act independently. They are linked by a neural ring, giving them the ability to communicate with each other without the involvement of the brain.

This means octopus's tentacles can make decisions on their own, and can still react to objects even when severed.

**219.
The average adult will walk almost 75,000 miles over their lifetime – the equivalent of traveling around the world three times.**

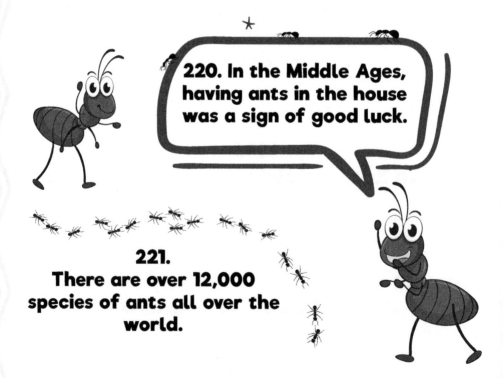

220. In the Middle Ages, having ants in the house was a sign of good luck.

**221.
There are over 12,000 species of ants all over the world.**

222. After You

The Yoruba people of Nigeria give birth to more twins than anywhere else in the world, at a rate of 50 per 1,000 births.

Twins are so common that traditionally they are given specific names. The first to be born is called Taiwo, meaning "the first twin to taste the world".

The second is called Kehinde, meaning "the second-born of the twins". Even though Taiwo is the firstborn, it is believed that Kehinde is the elder twin, having sent Taiwo into the world first to see if it is time to be born.

223. Webbed Wound

In ancient Rome, spider webs were used as bandages. Spider webs are naturally anti-fungal as well as antiseptic, useful for keeping wounds clean and preventing infections. It's also packed with vitamin K, which assists in blood clotting.

224. Blue Tooth

Bluetooth technology is named after a 10th-century Viking king. Harold "Blatand" Gormsson was the ruler of both Norway and Denmark from the year 958 to 985. His greatest accomplishment was uniting both countries under his rule.

Gormsson had a dead tooth which had a very dark blue shade to it, and the nickname Blatand translates from Danish to "Bluetooth."

The name was settled upon in 1996 when it was suggested by Intel representative Jim Kardash, the reasoning being that Bluetooth aimed to unite the PC and mobile phone industries.

225. Right to Rule

In late 1977, in an attempt to strengthen their claim on the frozen land, Argentina airlifted seven months pregnant Silvia Morella de Palma to Esperanza Base near the tip of the Antarctic Peninsula.

Emilio Marcos Palma was born on 7th January 1978 and is featured in the Guinness Book of Records as the first person in known history to be born on the continent.

226. The Man, the Myth

Leonidas I, the famous Spartan warrior at the head of the 300 that held back the Persian army at the Battle of Thermopylae in 480 B.C., wasn't quite as young as you might think. He was 60 years old when he fell in the battle before passing in to legend.

227. Closet Lodger

After becoming suspicious because food was mysteriously disappearing from his home, an unnamed resident of Kasuya, Japan, installed security cameras to see if he could find out what was going on.

Much to his surprise, he watched as a 58-year-old woman clambered out of his closet to steal his food. Later she was arrested, and it transpired that the homeless lady had been living in his house for a year.

228.
At 60 mph, it would only take one hour to drive to space.

229. If it ain't Broke

Twinings Tea has used the same logo continuously for 227 years, making it the world's oldest unaltered logo.

230. I Want to be Free

In certain countries such as Belgium, Germany and Mexico, attempting to escape from prison is perfectly legal and not punishable, as the laws recognize it is basic human nature to want to be free.

Prisoners who do flee, though, will be charged for any crimes committed while on the run, such as breaking windows or damaging metal bars.

231. An Apple a Day

If you're looking for a pick me up in the mornings, instead of reaching for the coffee, consider an apple. Depending on the size, apples can be packed with around 13 grams of natural sugar, which is a significant source of energy for the body.

232. Wing Warm Up

Butterflies need to maintain a body temperature of 86 F (30 C) in order to fly. If they become too cold, not only can they not fly, but they are rendered completely immobile.

Butterflies are cold-blooded and so they cannot regulate their own body temperature. To help them warm up for flight, they bask in the sun, staying still on vegetation with their wings spread in direct sunlight.

233.
Having multiple tattoos can strengthen the immune system.

234.
NASA's internet speed is 400 Gb/s, roughly 17,800 times faster than the fastest internet connections available to consumers.

235.
Two-thirds of the world's population has never seen snow.

236.
Sea Otters have a favorite rock, and they store it in a pouch under their arm.

237.
Sleeping under a weighted blanket can help reduce anxiety as well as bring about a deeper sleep.

238.
Portuguese is the official language of 9 countries.

239.
Lisbon is home to world's oldest bookstore.

240.
Portugal is the oldest country in Europe.

241.
Over half the world's cork comes from Portugal.

242.
Portugal and England have the oldest alliance in the world - signed in 1373.

243.
Portugal has its own genre of music known as "Fado."

244. Hot Hack

In 1999, a flaw was discovered in Hotmail that allowed anybody to log into any account using the password "eh". At the time, it was called "the most widespread security incident in the history of the web."

---

245. Hungry Hummer

Hummingbirds are incredibly hungry creatures that burn through their energy reserves fast. So fast, in fact, that a human would have to eat 300 hamburgers to match the equivalent of what they consume to survive every day.

---

246. Third Times a Charm

Pope Benedict IX is the only man to have been pope on more than one occasion, holding the title three times over his lifetime. He was first made pontiff in 1032 at around the age of 20, and in 1044 he was forced out of the city of Rome by his rivals due to his scandalous lifestyle.

His second pontificate began in 1045 after he managed to expel his rival, but ended in the same year after offering to give up the papacy if his election expenses were covered by his godfather John Gratian. The offer was accepted and Gratian became Pope Gregory VI.

Finally, in 1047, Benedict IX seized the Lateran Palace - the main papal residence at the time - again becoming pope, but was eventually driven away by German troops in 1048.

---

247. Land Migration

Due to various activities within the sea floor, America and Europe move 1.5 inches further apart each year. In other words, the Atlantic is slowly getting bigger, meaning that the Pacific is getting smaller.

248. Dreamt is the only word in the English language that ends in "mt".

249. Brief Battle

The shortest ever war was just thirty-eight minutes long. Following the death of his uncle, Khalid bin Bargash seized power and declared himself the Sultan of Zanzibar.

The British had their own plans and wanted a different ruler, Hamid bin Muhammed, as they viewed Khalid as far too independent. They issued an ultimatum at 8am, giving one hour for the new ruler to make way, which he declined.

At exactly 9am, five ships of the Royal Navy began bombarding the Royal Palace, and a force of marines landed on the shore. Khalid quickly fled to the German consulate and was quietly escorted out of the country.

Thirty-eight minutes later, the white flag of surrender was raised above the palace. Five hundred defenders died during the assault, compared to one British marine who was injured during the landing.

250. Violin bows are commonly made from horsehair.

251. Fine Work

Between the years of 1912 and 1948, the Olympic Games held competitions for sculpture, painting, music, architecture and literature.

252. Sacrilegious!

Forks were once considered to be blasphemous. They were first introduced in Italy in the 11th century but were seen as an offence to God because they represented artificial hands.

253. Love is Blind

When a person falls in love, the part of the brain responsible for making judgements about an individual becomes impaired, causing them to ignore flaws that others can easily see.

254. You Win!

When playing, male puppies will often let female puppies win, even if they have the upper hand. This is often accompanied with a play bow, all because the male just wants the playing to continue.

255. Imaginary Insects

The sensation of tiny insects crawling across the skin even though there is nothing there is known as "formication." The word derives from "formica," which is the Latin word for ant.

Sometimes formication is caused by static electricity attracting particulates - microscopic pieces of solid or liquid matter suspended in the air. These cause the body hair to move and can give the sensation of crawling insects.

256. Keep it to Yourself

People are statistically more likely to fail at their goals when they tell others about them. According to a study, being acknowledged for setting a goal makes people feel closer to having achieved it. This false proximity kills the momentum, and more often than not, the goal is never reached.

257. Bob

The current flag of the United States was designed by a 17-year-old high schooler.

Robert G. "Bob" Heft created the design as part of a school project in Lancaster, Ohio. He only received a B- from his teacher. Disappointed but not deterred, Bob made a deal with his teacher. They agreed that if the design were to become the flag of the US, he would get a better grade for the project.

Eventually, Heft's design was chosen out of more than 1,500 designs given to President Eisenhower, and the teacher duly changed his grade to an A.

258. Half Asleep

When we sleep in a new place, our brains go in to survival mode. Studies have shown that one hemisphere remains "awake" so that we are more alert to our surroundings and able to react if strange sounds are heard.

259.
Wearing headphones for an hour can increase the bacteria in your ear by 700 times.

260.
An avocado will never ripen on the tree.

261.
A cat's tail contains nearly 10% of all the bones in its body.

262.
The Nile crocodile can hold its breath for up to two hours while hiding underwater and waiting for its prey.

263.
All apes laugh when they are tickled.

264.
Almonds belong to the same family of plants as plums, cherries, and peaches.

265.
Tigers have striped skin, not just striped fur.

266.
Cockroach milk is three times as nutritious as cow's milk.

267.
"Deipnophobia" is the fear of dining or dinner conversations.

268.
Newborn children produce trace amounts of gold in their hair.

269.
The Mona Lisa was almost unheard of until it was stolen in 1911.

270. Seeing Spots

The little spots you sometimes see in your vision are known as "floaters." They are microscopic fibers inside your eye that cast shadows on your retina.

271. Snap Happy

With the invention of camera phones and easy accessibility, we take more pictures every two minutes than all of humanity did in the 19th Century.

272. Internal Chatter

Talking to yourself is not only incredibly normal, it has also been shown to increase cognitive performance. Encouraging yourself out loud has been shown to boost determination in the same way it would if someone else was cheering for you, and talking to yourself to calm down is also very effective.

273. Bad Ad Strategy

Movie trailers were originally shown after, or "trailing," a feature film, hence the name trailers. They were almost completely ineffective as audiences left straight after the picture had finished, so they were brought forward to be shown before anything else.

274.
No number before 1,000 contains the letter "A."

275. R'oh Deer!

Certain trees "know" when they are being eaten. When trees are "injured," such as a branch being snipped by a human or animal, they release hormones known as jasmonates. Not only do these chemicals help with the recovery process, but they are also released to communicate with other trees nearby. In response, the other trees elevate their defenses against disease, animals and insects.

However, trees studied in Leipzig, Germany, have displayed evidence to suggest they know what they are being attacked by, and are able to tailor their response.

When roe deer were observed nibbling on maple and beech branches, the trees released a second set of chemicals called salicylic acid which boosts protein production, allowing the trees to grow back what was lost, and bitter chemicals called tannins to make the tree distasteful and stop further feasting.

On the other hand, if a leaf or bud is snapped off with no animal involvement, the tree only produces the jasmonates.

276. Fluorescent Fungi

There are over 70 different species of mushroom that can glow in the dark. The bitter oyster mushroom is one of most dazzling, and even though it can be found all over the world, it is only in North America where you'll find the bright green fungi beaming at night.

277. Turkey God

In 300 B.C., turkeys were considered by the Maya as vessels of the gods. Domesticated and used in religious rituals, they were symbols of prestige and owned almost exclusively by the rich and powerful.

278.
Dogs can breathe in and breathe out at the same time.

279.
A dogs sense of smell is so good that they are able to sniff out many kinds of disease.

280.
The area in the brain of a dog responsible for detecting smells is 40 times larger than in humans.

281.
Dogs will normally start sniffing something with their right nostril to investigate, but if the smell is something pleasant, like food for example, they will switch to their left nostril.

282.
Dogs' noses are wet to help them determine smells. Their noses secrete a special mucus that absorbs scent chemicals, and they then lick their noses to sample them to understand what the smell is.

283. First Flight

The first hot-air balloon flight took place on 19th September 1783.

Joseph and Étienne Montgolfier, two brothers in Versailles, France, had been experimenting with lighter-than-air flight in 1782 and had caught the attention of the Académie Royale des Sciences, which then asked them to travel to Paris to repeat the experiments.

After seven days of testing and repairing, the brothers were ready to demonstrate their invention in front of Louis XVI and the royal family.

As a safety measure, animals were used in place of people. At 1 pm, a sheep, a cockerel and a duck were placed in to the round wicker basket and eleven minutes later a cannon was fired, signaling the lift-off of the basket.

The crowd, bewildered but blown away by what they were witnessing, rang out in rapturous applause. The balloon reached an incredible 1,968 feet (600 meters) in the air before a rip in the fabric forced it to descend eight minutes later. It traveled just over two miles and came to rest in the Wood of Vaucresson.

Completely against expectations, all the animals survived the flight, were hailed as heroes of the air and rewarded with a place at the Menagerie by Louis XVI.

Two months later, on 21st November 1783 at Château de La Muette, Pilâtre de Rozier became the first ever person in the history of mankind to leave the ground.

284. Magical Melody

Chills experienced when listening to music are caused by a chemical called dopamine, which is released by the brain and plays an important role in how we feel pleasure.

285. Something Something Smart

Being forgetful is a sign of intelligence. Research suggests that the brains of those with higher intellect optimized decision making by remembering valuable information and forgetting the less important details.

286. War on Cats

During the 13th century, Pope Gregory IV ordered the extermination of black cats across Europe as he believed the animals were the instruments of Satan. Unfortunately, things didn't work out too well as it resulted in an increase of plague-carrying rats.

287. Mucky Moisturizer

Due to the very high cost, Roman gladiators rarely fought to the death. They were incredibly popular and had some extremely fanatical followers. Some rich Roman ladies were so obsessed that they paid to have the muck and sweat scraped off of their favorite fighters after a session in the arena, which they would then use as a moisturizer.

288. Cracking!

When glass breaks, the cracks move at 3,000 mph. This is five times faster than the average airplane.

289. Laughing Legend

Legendary cosmologist Stephen Hawking went through a lot during his life, but he never lost his sense of humor.

During an interview at Cambridge University in 2004, the camera operator accidentally pulled a cable from its socket, causing an alarm to sound. Hawking slumped forward as if his life support had been switched off.

The crew panicked, thinking they had accidentally killed one of the world's greatest minds. As they rushed forward to help him, they found him giggling at his own joke, as the alarm was nothing more than an office computer losing power.

290. Military Marriage

Genghis Khan may have taken much territory by force, but he was also a dab hand at diplomatic conquest.

The shrewd warmonger would offer a daughter to the leader of an allied nation. He would then assign his new son-in-law to military duty in the Mongol Wars, where, more often than not, they would be killed in combat.

Upon their death, Khan's daughters would then be in complete control of the country. By the time he died, Genghis Khan's daughters ruled from the Yellow Sea to the Caspian (roughly South Korea to Georgia).

291. A single red blood cell can travel round the whole body in under 20 seconds.

292. Reely?

You can buy eel flavored ice cream in Japan. In fact, it has proved so popular that its creator now also produces ice cream made from sea slugs, whale meat, cedar chips and soft-shelled turtles.

293. Buzz Berry

Coffee as we know it is said to have been found in the year 800. The story goes that an Ethiopian goat herder named Kaldi discovered it when his goats became overly energetic after eating berries from a certain tree.

He reported his findings to the abbot of the local monastery, who then made a drink from the berries. The abbot found he was alert and unable to sleep, and so the knowledge of the energizing berries began to spread.

Soon after, word of the beverage found its way across the Arabian Peninsula, and eight centuries later spread its way to Europe.

294. Ancient Footwear

Sandals are the oldest form of footwear. The oldest pair still in existence were found at Fort Rock Cave in Oregon in 1938 by anthropologist Luther Cressman.

Cressman believed the sandals to be ancient, but as carbon dating was years away from being invented, he could not prove anything. When it was invented by Willard Libby in the 1950s, the sandals were found to be over 9,000 years old.

295. Pen & Paper

Although the invention of ink and paper is widely credited to the Egyptians, recorded history shows that both were invented by two Chinese men.

T'sai-Lun was a Chinese inventor and court official of the Eastern Han Dynasty. Although certain forms of paper had existed since the 3rd Century BCE, in the year 105, he was responsible for significant improvements in papermaking by adding new materials such as tree bark, hemp, rags and old fishnet.

During the Bronze Age several thousand years before, in 2697 B.C., a Chinese philosopher called Tien-Lcheu formulated a dark liquid for making ink by taking soot from pine wood and mixing it with oil used in lamps. Tien then made a gelatin by mixing the skin of a donkey with musk, and then combined it with the soot and the oil.

As time went on and this new ink became popular, people began mixing the ink with natural dyes and minerals to create different colors.

296. Old Secrets

The oldest known door lock is over 4,000 years old. It was discovered in Nineveh, an ancient Assyrian city in modern-day northern Iraq.

297. Now Watch This Drive

Golf is the only sport to have been played on the moon. In 1971, Alan Shepard hit two golf balls on the lunar surface with a makeshift 6-iron.

298. Praise the Pug

In Bavaria, 1738, Roman Catholics founded a secret society called the Order of the Pug. New members were initiated by being told to wear a dog collar and having to scratch at the door when they wanted to get in. They also had to kiss the backside of a porcelain pug under its tail as an expression of devotion to the order.

The order was eventually banned in 1748, however, they were reportedly active in Lyon as late as 1902.

299. Power Shrimp

The super bright and multicolored peacock mantis shrimp can throw a punch at 50 mph, accelerating its fist-like clubs quicker than a .22-caliber bullet. The shrimp doesn't have powerful muscles, but instead has arms that are spring-loaded, allowing it to smash its victims' shells to pieces.

300. A group of kangaroos is called a "mob."

301. Wetter Water

Firefighters use wetting agents to make water wetter. The chemicals reduce the surface tension of plain water so it's easier to spread and soak into objects, which is why it's known as "wet water."

302. Athletically Mechanical

Being a member of the pit crew in a NASCAR (National Association for Stock Car Auto Racing) team is so demanding that instead of hiring mechanics with athletic abilities, teams instead recruit competitive athletes who played a sport in college and then train them in mechanics.

303. Tasteless Travel

When flying at heights of 30,000 feet and above, our sense of smell and taste are reduced by as much as 30%. As the plane flies higher, the air pressure drops and humidity levels decrease significantly.

This combination of low pressure and dryness reduces the sensitivity of our taste buds to sweet and salty foods, possibly explaining why on-board food is not the greatest.

304. Sick Humor

Witzelsucht is a rare and uncontrollable condition in which the sufferer has continuous impulses to tell silly stories or make really terrible puns. Translated from German into English, witzelsucht means "joke addiction."

305.
Only two countries use the color purple in their national flags - Nicaragua and Dominica.

306.
Turkeys may attack or attempt to dominate humans they see as inferior.

307.
Candle flames contain millions of microscopic diamonds.

308.
A 100 lb woman wearing stilettos exerts 20 times more pressure on the ground than a 6000 lb elephant.

309.
Africa and Asia are home to nearly 90 percent of the world's rural population.

310.
A group of crows is called a "murder," and a group of lemurs is called a "conspiracy."

311.
The chainsaw was originally invented to be used in childbirth.

312.
The average person will spend 79 days of their life brushing their teeth.

313.
In Japan, Ronald McDonald is called Donald McDonald as it easier to pronounce in Japanese.

314.
The sea slug Elysia chlorotica is the first animal known to be part animal and part plant.

315. Angry Anchovy

Around 45 to 55 million years ago, there were saber-toothed anchovies that roamed the seas. One species discovered in Belgium was called Clupeopsis straeleni and measured just under 20 inches (50 cm) long.

The other was called Monosmilus chureloides, was discovered in Pakistan and was about 40 inches (100 cm) in length.

316.
The common cold virus originated in camels.

317.
Falling coconuts kill 150 people every year - ten times the number of people that are killed by sharks.

318. Bad Egg

Because American eggs are legally required to be washed and sanitized before they are sold, they are banned across the whole of Europe where laws state the eggs must remain unwashed.

European lawmakers believe this encourages good husbandry on farms and pushes farmers to produce the cleanest eggs possible.

319.
There are five species of rhino. Two - black and white rhinos - are from Africa. The other three - greater one-horned, Javan and Sumatran - are from Asia.

320.
White rhinos are the largest, and can weigh over 7700 pounds (3,500 kg).

321.
The name rhinoceros comes from the Ancient Greek words rhino (nose) and ceros (horn).

322.
Despite their incredible size, rhinos are capable of running between 30 - 40 miles per hour.

323.
Male rhinos are called "bulls," whereas female rhinos are called "cows." Young rhinos are known as "calves," and the collective term for a group of rhinos is a "crash."

324.
For every person in New Zealand, there are 9 sheep.

325.
The kiwi fruit is not actually native to New Zealand. It is from China, but was named after the bird.

326.
Bats are the only native land animals in New Zealand, the rest were introduced by Europeans and Maoris.

327.
The steepest residential street in the world is called Baldwin Street and has a gradient of 38 degrees.

328.
There are no snakes in New Zealand.

329.
When heated above 176 F (80 C), magnets will lose their magnetic properties.

330.
Mercury and Venus are the only two planets in our solar system that do not have any moons.

331.
Only 22 countries in the world have never been invaded by Britain.

332.
"Strengths" is the longest word in the English language with only one vowel.

333.
Abibliophobia is the fear of running out of things to read.

334.
The Sahara Desert is only 30% sand, the remaining 70% is mostly gravel.

335. Man's Best Friend

People that own dogs tend to live longer than those that do not. When interacting with dogs, humans get a jolt of oxytocin - the so-called cuddle hormone.

Research has shown that over a 12-year period, people with heart disease that hug dogs every day have a 21% reduction in the risk of death.

336. Looking for Something...

How many times have you walked in to another room only to forget why you are there?

This is known as the Doorway Effect. As we pass from one room to another, a mental block is created in the brain. When walking through a doorway, the memory is reset to make room for a new set of events to take place. This reset causes us to forget why we entered a room, what we were looking for or why we are staring in to a fridge.

337. Your Name, Sir?

The world-famous Spanish painter Picasso actually had a slightly longer name.

In its entirety, his full name was Pablo Diego José Francisco de Paula Juan Nepomuceno María de los Remedios Cipriano de la Santísima Trinidad Ruiz y Picasso.

338. Monkey Stonks

In 1999, a six-year-old chimpanzee named Raven became the 22nd most successful money manager in America after choosing stocks by throwing darts at a list of 133 companies.

Called MonkeyDex, the chimp's selection bore a 213% gain and outperformed more than 6,000 professional brokers on Wall Street.

339. Available - Small Country with Mountains

Rapper Snoop Dogg once tried to rent the entire country of Lichtenstein for one of his video shoots.

The tiny mountainous country wedged between Switzerland and Austria turned down the offer, but not because the idea was completely crazy. Karl Schwaerzler, a Lichtenstein property agent said, "It would have been possible, but Snoop Dogg's management did not give us enough time."

340. Hey Ju - Oh ****

In the famous Beatles song Hey Jude, if you listen carefully at the 2:58 minute mark, you can hear Paul McCartney swearing after making a mistake on the piano.

John Lennon is quoted as saying: "Paul hit a clunker on the piano and said a naughty word."

341. Feathered Friends

African gray parrots help their friends get food even though there's nothing in it for themselves. After being trained to exchange tokens for food when a human held out their hand, some parrots were given tokens and some were left without.

The ones with the tokens were observed handing them to their friends so that everyone could have something to eat, a behavior not common in many other bird species.

342. A Little Green Around the Gills

Motion sickness occurs because your brain thinks you have been poisoned. Even though a person is traveling in a vehicle and moving at a certain speed, as they are sitting still, they are technically stationary.

The brain knows that a forward motion is occurring due to the balance sensors in the inner ear, and as these little tubes of fluid slosh around, the brain receives mixed signals. The thalamus – the part of the brain that relays sensory impulses from receptors in various parts of the body to the cerebral cortex – is trying to make sense of this.

The conclusion it reaches is that you've been poisoned, and that is why vomiting occurs.

343.
Sea otters hold hands when they are asleep so they don't drift apart.

344. Married Martial Arts

Married couples in medieval Germany were able to legally settle their disputes by fighting a marital duel.

To make sure it was a fair, the husband had to fight from inside a hole with one arm tied behind his back, while his wife was free to move around and was armed with a sack full of rocks.

345. That Was my Idea!

Have you ever come out with something that sounds like an awesome saying, or had a great idea that you think is original, only to find out that it has already been said or done?

This is known as "cryptomnesia" and it occurs when a forgotten memory comes back to you without being recognized, and so you believe it to be new and original.

346. Red Spotted Spinner

Jupiter is the fastest spinning planet in our Solar System. The gas giant rotates once in just under 10 hours, meaning that Jupiter has the shortest days of all the planets in the Solar System.

347. Master of Words

William Shakespeare invented over 1,700 of the most common words in the English language. He did this by changing verbs into adjectives, nouns into verbs, connecting words not used together before, adding prefixes and suffixes and creating completely new words.

348. The Joy of Giving

The happiness we feel after an event or activity becomes less and less each time we experience that event – a phenomenon known as hedonic adaptation. One activity that isn't affected by this adaptation is the act of giving, which has been shown to cause the same level of happiness each time the action is performed.

349. Greenland Greats

Greenland sharks can live up to 500 years and maybe even slightly beyond, though the average is said to be around 392. The sharks grow at a rate of 10 millimeters a year and are the longest living vertebrates known on Earth.

350. Pyramid Pals

Egypt is known all over the world for its famous pyramids and has between 118 and 138, but its Northeast African neighbor Sudan has many more – over 200 pyramids.

The Sudanese pyramids are much smaller at roughly 20 to 98 feet (6 to 30 meters), while the average Egyptian pyramid is about 452 feet (138 meters).

351. Starfish have no brains and no blood.

352. Calorie Killer

Watching a horror film can burn just as many calories - around 150 - as a quick jog or a 30-minute walk. The scarier the film, the more calories are burned.

353. A Strangers Goodbye

If a person dies in the Netherlands with no next of kin, no family or friends and with no one to attend the funeral, a city poet writes a custom poem and attends that funeral so that nobody is alone the day they are buried.

The practice was started by poet Frank Starik and is known as The Lonely Funeral project.

354. Buffalo Debate

African buffalo herds decide which direction to travel in by having a vote.

The process involves the adult females of the herd standing up one by one, staring in a particular direction and then lying back down. The direction that gets the most looks is more often than not the way the herd travels.

If the vote is evenly divided, the herd will often split before one half follows the other.

355. Power Plant

The world's fastest growing plant belongs to a species of bamboo called Phyllostachys Atrovaginata - or Incense Bamboo. The plant can be found in the UK and has been recorded growing at a rate of just under 3 feet a day.

356. Drop of the Good Stuff

Originally found in 1867, the Speyer wine bottle is considered to be the world's oldest bottle of wine. It was found in a Roman tomb in Speyer, Germany, and has been dated between 325 and 350 AD.

357. Safe Travels

For a brief time on one road in Stockholm, Sweden, every time someone drove past a speed camera under the limit, they were entered into a lottery where the prize fund was made up from the fines of speeding drivers.

The biggest pay out was 20,000 krona – roughly $2,350 or £1,700.

358. Always Someone Bigger

Mount Everest is often thought to be the tallest mountain in the world, and while this is true above land, the tallest mountain on Earth is actually Mauna Kea, a dormant volcano in Hawaii.

Above the sea, Mauna Kea is only 13,803 feet (4,207 meters) whereas Everest is 29,032 feet (8,848 meters). If you include what is below the sea, however, Mauna Kea is 33,500 feet (10,210 meters), making the entire mountain over 4,000 feet (1,219 meters) taller than Everest.

359. Rent-a-Bear

Nearly all the pandas in the world are owned by the Chinese government. Zoos in America pay up to $1 million each year to rent just one. If any baby pandas are born during the length of the contract - usually 10 years - then the zoo is liable for a one-time tax of $400,000.

360. Slightly Chilly

In 1998, the coldest temperature ever on Earth was recorded in Antarctica. At -144 F (-98 C), just a few breaths of air would cause hemorrhaging in your lungs and kill you.

361. Papua Polyglot

12% of the world's total languages are found in Papua New Guinea, which has over 820 indigenous languages. There are more languages on this island than in any other country.

362. It's Flindrikin!

Scotland has more than 400 words and expressions for snow. A few examples include feefle, flindrikin, snaw-pouther, spitters and unbrak.

363. Zombie Plant

There exists a certain type of plant known as the resurrection plant that can survive for months without a drop of water. One such plant - Selaginella lepidophylla - also known as the "Rose of Jericho", is a resurrection plant native to the Chihuahuan desert of the US and Mexico.

During the dry season, the branches curl up, forming the plant into a dead-looking ball that can become uprooted and blown along the ground as tumbleweed. As soon as it comes in to contact with moisture, the ball will begin to revive itself, and over a few hours regain its green color.

The plant is able to survive such harsh conditions thanks to the presence of a sugar called trehalose that protects its cells from damage as a result of dehydration.

364.
Conspiracy theories are, on average, 70% more likely to be shared online than the truth.

365.
Water can dissolve more substances than any other liquid, including sulphuric acid.

366.
Cleopatra was not an Egyptian, she was Greek.

367.
During the 1830s, ketchup was sold as a medicine for indigestion.

368.
The human brain uses 20% of the body's oxygen.

369.
The longest river in all of Asia is called the Yangtze River. Located in China, it is 3,915 miles long.

370.
Charles Dickens had a fear of trains.

371.
The man who invented cruise control - Ralph Teetor - was blind.

372.
The singular of "confetti" is "confetto".

373.
It requires 7 to 8 trees to provide enough oxygen for one person per year.

374.
Holding money has been shown to reduce stress and pain.

375.
The word "checkmate" in chess comes from the Persian phrase "Shah Mat," which means "the King is dead."

376. Ancient Means

You may think of the guillotine as an ancient method of execution. Surprisingly, France only abolished the form of capital punishment as recently as 1981, with the last execution by such means taking place in 1977.

377. Mad Science

In 1813, French chemist Michel Bertrand mixed 5 grams of a very poisonous substance called arsenic trioxide with activated charcoal, before drinking the concoction in an effort to demonstrate the charcoals absorbent properties and application in medicine.

Fortunately for him, he was correct about the charcoal, and he survived his own poisoning.

378. Friends in Unlikely Places

Haiti was the first government in the world to recognize Greek independence after their revolution against the Ottoman Empire.

Some historians have claimed that Jean-Pierre Boyer, one of the leaders of the Haitian Revolution against French rule and President of Haiti from 1818 to 1843, sent the Greeks 25 tons of Haitian coffee to be sold in order to finance weapons.

379. American singer and composer Tim Storms can produce a note so low that humans are unable to hear it.

380. Ostrich Myth

Contrary to popular belief, ostriches do not bury their heads in the sand to escape danger. The only time an ostrich puts its head in the sand is when they use their beaks to rotate any eggs that they have laid.

381. Let's Dance

In 1518, a dancing plague broke out in Strasbourg, Alsace - today's modern-day France.

The outbreak started when a woman began to dance in the street. Historical documents from physicians and the city council clearly detail the strange event, though it is not known why it happened.

Experts agree that there was indeed a dance epidemic.
Some people danced for such a long time that eventually the magistrate, the bishop and a group of doctors intervened and put those affected in hospital.

382. Alarm Nail

Back in the days when clocks didn't exist, candle clocks were used that could be burned for a set number of hours.

People that needed to be up at certain times of the day would push a heavy nail in to the candle clock, so that when it melted to the correct time, the nail would fall and clank on a metal holder, waking the person up.

383.
The Mongolian stock exchange is located in an old children's cinema.

384.
Fermented horse milk is a popular Mongolian beverage. It's called Airag and has around 3% alcoholic content.

385.
Around a quarter of the Mongolian population live as nomadic herders.

386.
The sky in Mongolia remains cloudless for over two-thirds of the year, and the country is often referred to as "The Land of the Blue Sky."

387.
If you accidentally bump in to someone in Mongolia, it is customary to apologize by shaking their hand.

388.
The Sahara Desert was once inhabited by galloping crocodiles.

389.
People who procrastinate are more likely to suffer from insomnia.

390.
Every time you drink a glass of water there is a 99.9% chance that the water has passed through a dinosaur.

391.
Drinking coffee doesn't actually increase our levels of alertness, it simply reverses the effects we experience from caffeine withdrawal.

392.
A grizzly bear can bite down with so much pressure that it could crush a bowling ball.

393. Power Pumpkin

The world's biggest pumpkin was grown in Belgium by Mathias Willemijns, and weighed 2,624.6 pounds (1190.49 kg) – that's 129.6 pounds (58.78 kg) more than an Alfa Romeo sports car.

394. Hop Out of Dodge

The red-eyed tree frog will hatch early from its egg if it senses danger nearby. Found in Mexico and across South America, if the unhatched frogs sense the vibrations of a possible predator attack, they tremble in their eggs, releasing enzymes from their snouts that dissolve a hole in the egg's shell.

This rapid enzyme release allows the frog to hatch at a moment's notice and escape in seconds, while hatching under normal conditions takes much longer.

395. A Night to Remember

At 1:10 am on 9th May 1945, street parties broke out everywhere within the Soviet Union after radio broadcasts reported Germany had surrendered and World War II was over. The people celebrated so much that a mere 22 hours later, the Union's entire vodka supply had run out.

396. Every single clownfish is born a male, and the dominant male of a group will turn female when the female of that group dies.

397. Wait, That's Illegal!

There is a small coal-mining town in Norway called Longyearbyen where it is often said that it is illegal to die. The truth is that no such law exists, however if someone is terminally ill, then they are required to move away. The reason for this is there are no burials allowed in the town.

The decision to stop burials was brought about in 1950 when it was discovered that, thanks to the permafrost in the region, the bodies of people that died in the 1918 flu pandemic had not decomposed. Scientists fear that corpses may still contain live strains of the virus.

Longyearbyen does have a few of its own unique laws though. Cats are banned, there is a limit on how much alcohol an individual can purchase on a monthly basis, and anyone venturing outside is required to carry a rifle to protect themselves against polar bears.

---

398. $#!"

Instead of writing swear words in comics, newspapers and digital media, writers often use symbols in place of profanity, £@#!, for example.

A symbol used in this way is known as a "grawlix." The term was coined by a cartoonist called Mort Walker, although the use of sweary symbols had been common long before he came up with the word.

399.
Men can become cognitively impaired after talking to a woman they find attractive.

400. Prodigious Penguin

Around 40 million years ago, there was a species of penguin that stood at 6 feet tall and weighed in at 250 pounds (113 kg).

401. Russian Blue

In the Russian language there is no single word for the color blue, but rather specific words for different types of blue, such as light blue and dark blue.

402. Blinding!

By the time you reach the age of 60, your eyes will have been exposed to more light than would be released by detonating a nuclear bomb.

403. Dead Weight

A neutron star is the super-dense remains of a giant star that has run out of fuel and collapsed in on itself thanks to gravity. If it were possible to bring some of this star down to Earth, a teaspoonful of it would weigh about 6 billion tons.

404. Keeping it in the Family

The world's oldest hotel has been in operation since 705 AD. Founded by Fujiwara Mahito, the Nishiyama Onsen Keiunkan in Yamanashi, Japan, has been in the hands of the same family for 52 generations over 1,300 years.

405. Raining Jewels

Scientists have discovered that the atmospheres in Neptune, Uranus, Jupiter and Saturn have such extreme pressures that they can crystalize carbon atoms and turn them into diamonds. Yes, it can rain diamonds on other planets!

406. Norse Naming Convention

In Iceland, if you decide to name your baby with a forename that's not yet been used in the country and is not on the government's official list of 3,565 names, it must first be approved by the country's naming committee. The aim is to preserve the language, which is close to Old Norse.

407. Not as Clever as You Think

A sophomaniac, or a person suffering from sophomania, is an individual who suffers from the delusion of having superior intelligence and thinking they are a lot smarter than they actually are.

408. Afterburn

Everybody knows that a candle wick is called a candle wick. But did you know the burned part of the wick after it has been lit is called the "snaste?"

409. "Lethologica" is a word used to describe that moment when you are mid conversation but find yourself unable to recall a specific word.

410. Littler Lung

As you grow older, your lungs naturally grow with the rest of your body. Your left lung, however, will always be slightly smaller than your right in order to make space for your heart.

411. Brain Freeze

The sharp pain a person feels in their head when eating or drinking something cold is commonly referred to as "brain freeze." The scientific term for this common and unpleasant experience is "Sphenopalatine Ganglioneuralgia."

It is caused when a group of nerves behind the nose called the sphenopalatine ganglion nerves come in to contact with something cold, such as icy cold water or ice cream.

Researchers theorize these nerves are highly sensitive to pain in order to protect the brain from any potential injury. It is also thought the pain itself is caused by an increase in blood flow to the brain, though scientists admit that further research is needed to fully understand the cause of the brain freeze sensation.

412. One Step Ahead

A type of sea slug called Elysia cf. marginata has been found by ecologists at Nara Women's University in Japan to not only survive decapitation, but to actually be able to regrow its body.

The severed slug heads continued to feed once removed, and after about 20 days, one third of the slugs had brand new bodies, including the heart and other organs.

413. Thirsty Threads

It takes around 700 gallons of water to make a single cotton shirt. For comparison, the amount of water needed to make one t-shirt is enough for one person to stay hydrated for 900 days.

414. Hairy Defense

Goosebumps are a physiological reaction whereby the hairs on our body stand on end. This ability is inherited from our ancestors, who had much more body hair than we do today, and was a way of retaining heat. In times long since passed when humans were prey, the hair standing on end was also a way of appearing bigger in order to help ward off predators.

415. Fast Glass

Because of the incredibly high temperatures, glass can form in sand instantly if lightning strikes it.

416. Madagascar Miniature

In January 2021, the smallest reptile on earth was discovered in northern Madagascar.

The miniscule male chameleon known as the Brookesia nana, or nano-cameleon, has a body of just 13.5mm, while its entire length from top to tail is 22mm. The female was found to be much bigger at around 29mm long.

Its primary source of food comprises of mites, and in order to hide from predators, it conceals itself in long blades of grass.

417. Wojtek the Brown Battle Bear

In 1942, during World War II, Polish prisoners were released from forced labor camps in Siberia. Free, but many, many miles away from home, the released prisoners traveled on foot to various destinations across Europe.

After a treaty was signed between the Soviet Union and Poland, commander Wladyslaw Anders was able to form a Polish Army, the 22nd Company, on Soviet soil. Eventually the army was cut off by the Soviet authorities due to a lack of food, and so the army marched to join the British in the Middle East.

On route, the soldiers had a chance encounter with a hungry shepherd who ended up trading his burlap sack for a Swiss army knife, a bar of chocolate and a tin of beef. Inside the sack was a tiny bear cub recently orphaned by hunters. The soldiers were so taken with their new friend that they made him the company mascot before settling on the name Wotjek – short for Wojciech, meaning "joyful warrior."

The bear was weaned on to condensed milk fed from an empty vodka bottle and assigned a caretaker named Peter Prendys, who had also been separated from his family during the conflict. Prendys taught the bear how to march, wave and salute while occasionally disciplining him when he stole from the provisions tent.

During downtime, Wotjek would hang around camp begging for food, racing the camp dog and climbing trees. He took a liking to cigarettes that he would puff on before eating them whole and also developed a taste for beer. He even once stole an entire clothesline's worth of women's underwear!

He wasn't afraid to pull his weight, though. On one occasion, he caught a spy trying to infiltrate the camp, and during the battle of Monte Cassino in Italy, Wotjek helped the soldiers carry crates of shells from trucks to the battle line.

The allies won the battle, the largest European land battle of the entire war, and was the cause of over 60,000 casualties. Stories of Wotjek spread far and wide, and the 22nd company honored their mascot by drawing up a new regalia featuring a silhouette of the bear carrying an artillery shell.

For the rest of his time in Italy, Wotjek developed a taste for hunting horses, dancing, and scaring people swimming on the Adriatic Coast.

After the war ended, he and his fellow soldiers ended up in Scotland at the Winfield Camp for Displaced Persons. There, he became a local celebrity and a massive comfort for other displaced people. His camp mates showed him lots of love by building him a swimming pool and taking him on field trips to local dances, where he listened calmy to fiddles being played as well as keeping a close eye on the baked goods table.

Wotjek found the time to drink two bottles of beer a day and continued to work as a laborer by helping to carry fenceposts through the Scottish fields alongside fellow farm workers.

As time went on, Wotjek's comrades in arms moved on, either settling permanently in Scotland or moving off to distant shores. His home was the camp that was slowly dismantling before him, and with much sorrow, his caretaker Prendys arranged for him to be sent to Edinburgh Zoo.

The bear's spirit waned in captivity even though he had many visitors. For the rest of his days Wojtek's comrades visited him regularly, talking to him in Polish, tossing him lit cigarettes and occasionally jumping in to the cage to wrestle with him.

Wotjek died at Edinburgh Zoo in 1963 at the age of 22. Today, a 10ft bronze sculpture can be found in Edinburgh depicting four scenes from Wotjek's life and the brave soldiers that accompanied him on his amazing journey.

418. A Fight to the Birth

It has been discovered that the developing embryos inside the wombs of pregnant sharks cannibalize each other. The last standing embryo is the largest, and having eaten all of its siblings, ensures the baby shark is born at a decently large size in order to make it safer against predators.

The process is known as intrauterine cannibalism, and occurs when developing baby sharks belonging to different fathers compete for survival.

419. Salt in the Wound

The first ever cell phone call was made in 1973 by Martin Cooper, a researcher and executive at Motorola at the time.

The person he called was Dr. Joel Engel, his chief competitor at AT&T, who also happened to be working on the "world's first cell phone."

The newly developed phone weighed over 2 pounds (1 kg) and had 20 minutes worth of talk time, before needing a 10-hour recharge.

420. First Defense

British doctor Edward Jenner created the first ever vaccine in 1796, and was developed in order to protect against smallpox. Jenner demonstrated that an infection with the much milder cowpox virus helped the body defend itself against the deadlier variant.

421. Must Sleep, Can't Sleep

Orthosomnia is a condition in which a person becomes so obsessed with getting a good night's sleep that they actually lose sleep over it.

422. There are around 900,000 species of insects on Earth, and at any given time there are an estimated 10 quintillion (10 followed by 18 zeros) alive and well.

423. Paper Saw

Paper cuts hurt a lot more than knife cuts due to paper being incredibly rough on a microscopic level. Knives tend to make straight cuts, while paper saws more like a blade, causing more damage to the nerve endings and skin cells.

424. The Elixir of Flying Fire

In their quest to create life-extending elixirs, Chinese monks were the first to discover gunpowder around the year 850. Texts dated from the 9th century state that "smoke and flames result, so that hands and faces have been burned, and even the whole house where they were working burned down."

The new powder was put to use by the ruling Sung dynasty against the Mongols to deter their continuing invasions into Chinese territory.

425. Death Breath

The Dragon's Breath chili pepper was developed to be used in medical treatment as an anesthetic that can numb the skin. However, it is so hot that if eaten, it could cause anaphylactic shock, burn the airways and completely close them up, causing an agonizing death.

426. The Living Dead

A parasitic fungus in the Amazon rainforest called Ophiocordyceps unilateralis has been found to infect foraging ants through spores that attach and penetrate the insect's exoskeleton.

Once infected, the ant will leave its nest to find a more humid climate suited to the fungus. Once there, the tiny creature will sink its jaws in to the vein of a leaf.

As the insect slowly dies, the fungus feeds on the innards of the ant. Several days after death has occurred, the fungus sends a fruiting body out through the base of the ant's head, and turns its host into a base from which it can spray its spores and infect new ants.

The fungus essentially controls the nervous system once it has taken hold, creating zombie ants.

427. Immortalized

The DNA sequence of Stephen Hawking is stored on a hard disk called the Immortality Drive and is onboard the ISS. He was among a select group of humans to have their DNA immortalized.

428. In a Flap

During direct flight, a hummingbird can beat its wings between 10 and 80 times per second. During a courtship dive, a male hummingbird can beat his wings up to 200 times per second in an effort to gain a female's attention.

429. New Forest

Every time a baby girl is born in the Indian village of Piplantri, the villager's plant 111 trees. This custom was started by former village leader Shayam Sundar Paliwal to honor his daughter, who sadly died at a very young age.

430. The Whiskey War

The Whisky War is a somewhat playful border conflict between Canada and Denmark over a place called Hans Island. Since the 1930s, the island has been a source of disagreement between the two nations.

Located in the middle of the Kennedy Channel between Greenland and Ellesmere Island, Hans Island has a theoretical line straight down the middle. Canada and Denmark could not come to terms on the issue in 1973 when a border treaty was signed, and it has been a source of contention since.

In 1984, the Canadians planted their flag on the island and left a bottle of bottle whisky behind. The Danes responded by planting their own flag and leaving a bottle of Snaps along with a letter stating "Welcome to the Danish Island."

The issue remains unresolved to this day.

431. Nectar Lock-On

Nectar guides are patterns which cause the center of flowers to appear darker under ultraviolet light. While invisible to the human eye, these patterns are visible to bees and other pollinators, making the flowers appear very different to them.

The nectar guides bring insects to the center of the flower, allowing them to pick up nectar and pollen.

432. Coffee Cam

The world's first webcam was created to monitor a coffee pot at Cambridge University. The last photo the webcam took was in 2001, when the computer department moved. The photo showed the server being switched off.

433. Serious Serpent

The venom of the Australian Brown Snake is so powerful that only 1/14,000th of an ounce is enough to kill a human.

These slithering beasts can exceed 6 feet (2 meters) in length and, on hot days, can move surprisingly fast.

434. Swimmy Sloth

Most species of Sloth are fantastic swimmers. Sloths can slow their heart rate so that they can hold their breath for much longer than usual - up to 40 minutes at a time, which is 4 times longer than the average dolphin.

435.
A lion's roar can be heard from 5 miles away (just over 8 km).

436.
It is estimated that there are only around 20,000 lions left in the wild.

437.
A fully grown lion can weigh 420 lbs (190 kg), and a lioness almost 280 lbs (127 kg).

438.
Male lions are responsible for defending a pride's territory while females do the hunting. Despite this, the males eat first.

439.
A lion's tongue is as rough as sandpaper. It is covered in tiny spines, called papillae, which are used to scrape meat from bones.

The tongue is so rough that a few licks on the back of a human hand would remove the skin.

440. Canine Clock Watch

Dogs can tell the time by using their sense of smell. They can gauge the time of day and how long their owner has been gone by how much their scent fades as the hours pass by.

441. President Bachelor

James Buchanan, the 15th President of the United States, is the only president to have come from Pennsylvania, and is also the only president that never married.

442. Mort Gage

The word mortgage is a French Law term meaning "death contract." While that may sound harsh, it simply means the contract dies when either the obligations are met or the property is taken through foreclosure.

443. Rain in the Air

When it rains, you may have noticed there is often a scent in the air, but rain itself doesn't have a scent at all. What you can smell is a combination of fragrant chemical compounds, and this earthly fragrance is known as "petrichor."

As raindrops land on different porous surfaces, air from the pores form in to small bubbles and releases aerosols. These aerosols carry the scent and bacteria from the soil.

Some scientists believe the reason we humans enjoy the smell of rain is because our ancestors may well have relied on rainy weather in order to survive.

444. Snow White and Awful

Snow White's seven dwarf companions originally had very different names. They were: Chesty, Burpy, Wheezy, Hickey, Tubby, Deafy and Awful.

445. Criminal Livestock

During the Middles Ages and up to as recently as the 18th century, many animals and insects in Europe were put on trial in court for various crimes.

Snakes, flies, rodents and other pests were often found guilty in religious courts and were banished from the land, and in some cases, even excommunicated. Criminal courts tried other larger animals, with one record in 1386 of a pig being dressed in human clothing before being hung for murder.

446. Scent of Stress

The pleasant scent released after mowing the lawn is actually a distress chemical given off by plants in trouble. Scientists believe these chemicals are used to attract nearby creatures that can help save the grass from attacks.

For example, when certain plants are being eaten, they release a chemical known as green leaf volatiles to attract nearby predators that attack and feed on the threat.

447. The tiny blob of toothpaste that you put on a toothbrush is called a "nurdle."

448. Vena Amoris

The tradition of wearing a wedding ring on your left finger goes all the way back to Ancient Rome. The Romans believed a vein ran from the fourth finger on the left hand all the way to the heart.

The vein is known as Vena Amoris which translated from Latin means "vein of love." Despite the romantic connotations, the vasculature in the human hand is pretty much all the same and there is no one vein that links directly to the heart.

449. Bucket of Blood, Anyone?

The tomato juice-based drink Bloody Mary wasn't always called Bloody Mary. Originally it was known as A Bucket of Blood and then Red Snapper, before finally settling on the name we know today.

450. Collateral State

Hawaii was not a US state when it was attacked by the Japanese on 7th December 1941. It wasn't until 18 years later, on 21st August 1959, that it went from being a US territory to the 50th state.

451. Someone who finds peace of mind and joy when it rains is known as a "pluviophile."

452. Back to the Fridge

The smash hit film series Back to the Future saw the main characters Marty and Doc traveling through time in a DeLorean car. In the original concept, the time machine was a refrigerator, but this was changed due to fears of children climbing in to fridges to try and travel back in time.

453. Monkey Snub

Towards the end of the 18th century, the phrase "you are a thief and a murderer and you have killed a baboon and stolen his face" was a very common way of insulting someone in Victorian England.

454. Polite Refusal

In 1952, Israeli Prime Minister David Ben-Gurion offered Albert Einstein the presidency on the conditions that he moved to Israel and accepted Israel as his nationality.

Einstein turned down the offer, stating, "I am deeply moved by the offer from our State of Israel, and at once saddened and ashamed that I cannot accept it. All my life I have dealt with objective matters, hence I lack both the natural aptitude and the experience to deal properly with people and to exercise official functions."

455. Dan the Music Man

Before writing books such as the well-known title The Da Vinci Code, Dan Brown had an unsuccessful attempt at being a pop star. Working as a singer and songwriter in Los Angeles, one of his albums, Angels & Demons, carried the same title as his bestseller released in 2000.

456. Blue From Brown

Vladimir Pravik was one of the first firefighters to reach the Chernobyl Nuclear Power Plant on 26th April, 1986. The radiation was so strong from the blast that his eye color changed from brown to blue.

457. Story Foreteller

Morgan Robertson was an American author of short stories and novels. One of his books, called Futility, was a story about an unsinkable ship named Titan that hit an iceberg in the Northern Atlantic.

14 years later, the Titanic sunk.

458. Baked Under Duress

Hanns Scharff was a master interrogator for the Germans during World War II. Instead of coercing his subjects by using threats or force, he would get his information by taking prisoners on nature walks, drinking beer with them, cracking jokes and baking cakes.

459. Buried Below

The famous Easter Island heads found in the South Pacific aren't just heads, they have hidden buried bodies below. As time has passed on Earth, the torsos have become buried in rock, preserving the rest of the unseen statue parts in all their glory.

460.
There are at least 70 uncontacted tribes in the Brazilian Amazon.

461.
Brazil has the world's longest stretch of continuous coastline, spanning 4,655 miles.

462.
Brazil was the last country in the Americas to abolish slavery in 1888.

463.
Brazil is the fifth-largest country in the world by land area.

464.
Around 60% of the Amazon rainforest is in Brazil.

465. Intelligent Sleeping

Several studies have shown that people who stay up later and wake up later are more creative and tend to have higher IQs.

466. Hum to Health

Scientists in America in 2002 discovered that humming is a good way to fight off sinus infections. Studies found that humming increased a gas called nasal nitric oxide by 15 times. Since reduced airflow is a major factor in sinus infections, the rapid exchange of this gas between the sinuses can help maintain healthier nasal cavities.

467. Runaway Science

When helium is cooled down to absolute zero, the lowest temperature possible (-460 F or -273 C), it becomes a liquid that flows against gravity. If you were to put some in a glass, it would start running up the sides and begin escaping over the edge.

468. Emotionally Decisive

The prefrontal cortex, the part of the human brain responsible for rational decision making, doesn't fully mature until we're about 25 years old.

Before that, we process information with the amygdala, the emotional part of the brain.

469. "Borborygmus" is another word for the sound of a grumbling tummy.

470. Oceanic Oxygen

Many people believe most of Earth's oxygen comes from trees, plants, and rainforests, but in fact between 50 – 80% of it is produced from oceanic plankton such as drifting plants, bacteria and algae.

471. From Bells to Boats

Alexander Graham Bell is more often than not associated with the invention of the telephone. He was, however, also responsible for the creation of a boat that went on to set a water speed record that remained unbeaten for 10 years. Helped in his work by his assistant Casey Baldwin, the two of them created a vessel that was capable of reaching 70.86 mph.

472. There Are No Words

Spain, Bosnia and Herzegovina, San Marino and Kosovo are the only four nations in the world that have no lyrics in their national anthems.

473. The Big Orange

When the Dutch captured New York from the English in 1673, they renamed it to New Orange in honor of William III of the House Orange. The English regained control the following year under the Treaty of Westminster and quickly removed the "Orange."

474. Australia is wider than the moon.

475. The Bigger Picture

1,000-piece jigsaw puzzles almost never have the exact number of pieces stated on the box. The vast majority of these puzzles are 38 pieces wide by 27 pieces high – 1,026 total.

476. Heavy Data

Adding data to electronic storage devices makes them weigh more. Information stored to computer memory, flash memory and SSDs requires storing an electric charge. Each electron carries with it a tiny amount of weight, so adding many electrons means adding more weight.

A full device with a capacity of 10 gigabytes would roughly weigh 7300 femtograms more than a device holding no data. For reference, a femtogram is less than 0.000000000000001 kilograms, so you would never know the difference.

477. Kitchen Chemistry

A Swedish man was arrested in 2011 on charges of unauthorized possession of nuclear material after trying to split atoms in his kitchen. Richard Handl claimed he had always been interested in physics and chemistry and had just wanted to see if it was possible to split atoms at home.

It was only after some time he realized what he was doing might not be legal, so he sent a letter asking Sweden's radiation authority, who in turn sent the police. Handl was eventually released and fined 13,600 Swedish kroner - about $1,540 today (£1,140 or €1335).

478. Oldest of Old Timers

The oldest person to have ever lived that could be verified was Jeanne Calment of France, who lived to the age of 122 years and 164 days (1875 - 1997).

479. Taking the Mickey

Computer mouse movements are measured in "mickeys." One mickey is the smallest movement and equals 1/200th of an inch, or just over 0.1mm. The speed of a mouse is measured in mickeys-per-second, and the sensitivity is measured in mickeys-per-inch.

480. Word Play

A word that describes itself is known as an autological word. For example, the word "short" is short, the word "English" is English, the word "word" is a word and the word unhyphenated is... unhyphenated.

The opposite of an autological word is a heterological word. For example, the word "long" isn't long at all.

481. Belly Bacteria

It is well known that all humans have individual fingerprints, but we also have unique belly button ecosystems as well. Different bacteria combinations live in each person, and scientists have discovered at least 1,458 new bacteria species only using belly button material.

482. In the municipality of Caldari di Ortona, Italy, there is a free 24-hour red wine fountain.

483. Ride on Time

Japanese trains are regarded as some of, if not the most punctual trains in the world. If a train in Japan is running over five minutes late, customers are issued certificates that can be shown to employers and schools to explain any late attendance.

484. Atomic Gamble

On July 19th, 1957, five officers from the US Air Force stood together on a small patch of ground northwest of Las Vegas as two F-89 jets flew towards their location. As the jets approached, one of them fired a 2-kiloton nuclear missile carrying an atomic warhead, which was then detonated directly above where the men were standing.

The aim of the exercise was to calm people's fears of nuclear fallout by showing that it was safe to use atomic weapons to counter similar weapons being developed in Russia. All the men lived in to their 70s and 80s.

485. Rock on, and on, and on...

The longest concert ever played took place in Canada to celebrate the country's 150th anniversary. Starting in Ontario on 17th March and finishing on 5th April, the gig lasted an impressive 437 hours and 54 minutes.

486. Forbidden Obscenities

Swearing during a tennis match at Wimbledon is not only frowned upon, it is strictly forbidden. In order to ensure all competitors stick to the rules, tennis umpires learn multiple swear words in multiple languages.

487. Turning Water in to Water

The British aircraft carrier HMS Elizabeth has a £1 million reverse osmosis system on board that draws in sea water and converts it in to 540 tons of fresh water every day.

488. The Tower of Silence

Zoroastrianism is an ancient religion still practiced today by around 150,000 worldwide. One of the more notable traditions associated with Zoroastrians are their funerals, where they lay their dead on top of a purpose-built tower called a dokhma, or Tower of Silence, in order to be exposed to the sun and eaten by birds of prey.

Zoroastrians believe that as soon as the body breathes its last breath, it becomes impure. Death is believed to be the work of an evil spirit known as Angra Mainyu, and contamination of the elements by burying a rotting corpse is considered sacrilege.

489. Put a Pillow on the Fridge

May 29th is the date of a peculiar tradition that sees observers place pillows on their fridge. Known as "Put a Pillow on Your Fridge Day," it is a tradition that goes back to the early 1900s. Families would place a piece of cloth typically found in the bedroom inside their larder, more commonly known today as the pantry. It was believed that placing these items where people kept their food would bring good fortune and prosperity to the household.

490. The flashes of light you see when you rub your eyes are known as "phosphenes."

491.
The odds of getting a royal flush in poker are exactly 1 in 649,740.

492.
There are no muscles in the fingers to control movement. They are moved entirely by forearm muscles and tendons.

493.
Frank Oz, the man behind the famous voice of Star Wars' Yoda, is also the voice of Miss Piggy.

494.
When combined, Americans spend more money on pets each year than Germany does on its entire defense budget.

495.
Flamingos are naturally white birds. They get their reddish-pink color from the pigments of the algae they eat as well as their healthy diet of brine shrimp.

496. Day of the Dead

The Day of the Dead is a holiday mostly observed in Mexico that takes place every year on the 1st and 2nd of November. The tradition goes back some 3,000 years, and involves family members of departed souls placing food, drink and tools to aid the deceased on a hard journey that takes place in the Land of the Dead, a place known as Chicunamictlán.

The journey through this land is said to be a challenging series of nine levels and takes a person several years to complete, but once overcome, the soul reaches Mictlán, the final resting place.

Until recently, the Day of the Dead had no street celebrations or parade, but such a thing came in to being thanks to the 2015 James Bond film Spectre. The film features a sequence of massive celebrations in Mexico City, and one year later, thanks to huge interest in the film and the government's wish to promote Mexican culture, authorities organized a "Día de Muertos" parade which was attended by 250,000 people.

497. Solar Nation

In the southern Pacific Ocean is a small island territory of New Zealand called Tokelau. The primary language there is Tokelauan, it has a population of just over 1,500, has the smallest economy of any nation and is the only territory in the world to be 100% solar powered.

498. Brain Power

One of the most widely believed things about the human brain is that we only use 10% of it. In reality we use 100% when we're awake, and then only 10% when we're asleep.

499. Bang, Peace!

Swedish inventor Alfred Bernhard Nobel, founder of the Nobel Peace Prize, was also responsible for inventing dynamite and other explosives.

500. Bouncy Glass

A ball made from glass will bounce higher than a ball made from rubber, assuming the glass ball doesn't break.

When a rubber ball hits a surface, its shape changes significantly. Quite a large amount of energy is lost as the ball returns to its original shape, whereas most of the energy from a glass ball bouncing returns to the glass, causing it to bounce higher.

501. Elaine Esposito

On August 6th 1941, a 6-year-old girl called Elaine Esposito went in to hospital for an appendectomy, a routine surgery procedure to remove the appendix if it is infected.

Elaine was administered general anesthetic, and instead of waking up after the procedure was complete, she stayed in a coma for 37 years and 111 days. Sadly, she never woke up and died in 1978.

502. Record for the Records

The Guinness Book of World Records is the most stolen book from public libraries, making it the record holder for the most stolen book.

503. Lunar Allergy

Geologist Harrison Schmitt, the last man to walk on the moon in 1972 during the Apollo 17 mission, landed on the moon only to find he was allergic to moon dust.

504. Intestune

The strings of instruments like the violin were once made with the intestines of animals that were available locally to makers.

505. Under the Drought

An ancient Native American people who dwelled in modern day New Mexico survived harsh droughts by melting the ice in lava tubes deep underground.

Known as Ancestral Puebloans, geoscientists discovered left behind charred material dating as far back as AD 150, showing that the natives took to the underground to survive the heat.

506. Like a Fish Out of Water

There is a fish native to parts of Africa and Asia known as the snakehead fish. What sets this particular fish apart from others is its ability to travel up to a quarter of a mile on land. Snakeheads have both gills and a special chamber next to their gills called a suprebranchial organ that allow them to breathe oxygen while out of the water.

Although native to two continents on the other side of the world, snakeheads have been found in the US recently for the first time, and with no natural predators to keep the numbers down, their numbers are booming.

507. Thirsty Flying

When on a flight, the human body loses about 8% of its water thanks to the humidity in the climate-controlled environment.

508. One Man Palais

A palace in Hauterives, France, called Le Palais Idéal, was built by a postman with no architectural knowledge whatsoever. Ferdinand Cheval spent 33 years of his life building his dream home, beginning in 1879, when he was 43 years old.

Cheval picked up any stones he could find during his mail round and would carry them back, before eventually acquiring a wheelbarrow to carry larger amounts. He spent many hours at night on the construction, working only by the dim light of an oil lamp.

The giant building still stands to this day and is visited regularly by sightseers.

509. Posh with a Pineapple

In 18th-century England, pineapples were a sign of wealth. One pineapple at the time would have cost around £60, roughly £5,000 in today's money ($6800).

The fruit was so highly regarded that it was possible to rent and show off pineapples at parties as status symbols.

510.
Some tarantula species can live without food for up to 2 years as long as they have a water supply.

511.
There are over 1,000 different species of tarantula belonging to the large spider family known as Theraphosidae.

512.
Male tarantulas may live as long as 10 to 12 years, whereas females have been known to live for 30 years.

513.
The Goliath birdeater can weigh as much as a very young puppy, and its leg span can reach up to 1 foot (30 cm).

514.
A spider-hunting wasp called the tarantula hawk actively seeks out the spider in order to reproduce.

The large wasp stings a tarantula to paralyze it before laying a single egg on its body, before sealing its victim in a burrow where the newborn feeds off the still-living but paralyzed spider.

515. Lovely Bubbly

If a bottle of sparkling wine or champagne has lost its fizz, dropping a single raisin in there will bring back the bubbles.

Once the raisin is in the bottle, the remaining carbon dioxide clings to the grooves of the little fruit and then releases back in to the bottle, bringing the beverage back to life.

516. Human teeth are as strong as shark teeth.

517. Not an Excuse

Although many people don't appreciate it, studies have shown that people who swear are often more honest and are likely to have higher intelligence. Swearing can also help people tolerate pain better, in addition to relieving stress.

518. Golden Sea

The ocean holds around 20 million tons of gold. It is spread so far and wide, however, that each liter of seawater only contains about 13 billionths of a gram. If it were possible to round it all up, every person on the planet would be able to have nine pounds of gold.

519. When the moon is directly overhead, you will weigh around 0.5 grams less than you normally do.

520. Baby Comfort

Baby elephants suck their trunks the same way baby humans suck their thumbs. They also do it for the same reason - comfort.

521. Treedom

There are more trees on earth than there are stars in the Milky Way. Estimates put the number of trees on our planet at around 1 trillion, while scientists think there are between 200 - 400 billion stars in our galaxy.

522. Sir Penguin

In 2008, a penguin living in Edinburgh Zoo received a knighthood. Sir Nils Olav III is a king penguin and the mascot to the King of Norway's guard. He was awarded the honor to celebrate the relationship between Scotland and Norway.

523. Slow Eater

Sloths have the slowest digestion rate of any mammal. They have a four-chambered stomach that accounts for 30% of their body mass, and it takes them 30 days to digest a single leaf.

524. Eye Can Help!

Frogs can't keep their eyes open when they swallow because they use them to help gulp down food. A frog's tongue isn't anchored to the back of its mouth, so instead their eyes sink in to the skull to put pressure on the food they're swallowing.

525. Crash Repair

A British soldier by the name of Hugh Trenchard became partially paralyzed when he was shot in the spine and chest during the Boer War. To help him recover, he traveled to Switzerland to rest and recuperate. While practicing his new hobby of bobsledding, Trenchard had a serious accident that left him unconscious. The crash managed to readjust his spine, and when he woke up, he was able to walk with no help at all.

Trenchard went on to win the St. Moritz Tobogganing Club's Freshman and Novices' Cups for 1901, and later that year was able to return to active duty in South Africa.

526. Blue Eyed Creator

After studying the DNA of people with blue eyes from Turkey, India and Scandinavia, researchers found that all of them have identical gene sequences for eye color. It is believed that this trait comes from a single person who lived 6,000 - 10,000 years ago, and carried with them a genetic mutation that has now spread across the world.

527. Extreme Ironing

Inspired by his brother-in-law John Slater, a man named Tony Hiam invented the sport of extreme ironing in 1980. Sometimes done by a solo competitor and sometimes as part of a team, extreme ironing has taken place in forests, in canoes, under sheets of ice and even while parachuting or bungee jumping.

528. Morbid Memories

During the first half of the 19th century, photography became an exciting invention that piqued much curiosity. For Victorians, it played a very important role in dealing with the passing of loved ones.

Most Victorians didn't live past 40 years old, so they used photography as a way of remembering their dead. Dressing recently deceased relatives - more often than not children - they would pose them in chairs and take pictures. The photographers would then add a pink tint to the cheeks of the person in the photo to give the impression they were still alive.

529. Bubble Wrapped

In 1957, engineers Alfred W. Fielding and Marc Chavannes sealed two shower curtains together, trapping some air in the process, and then tried to sell the result as wallpaper. Several years later, in 1960, they realized the air bubbles they had trapped inside the two curtains could be used for protection in packaging.

The pair went on to found the Sealed Air Corporation, and some time later they showed their product to IBM - who then became the first big bubble wrap customer.

530. Cloud Cover

Cloud cover is measured in units called oktas, and one okta is one eighth of the sky dome covered by cloud. Zero oktas mean not a cloud in the sky. One okta is a cloud amount of 1 eighth or less, seven oktas is almost complete cover, and eight oktas is full cloud cover with no breaks.

531.
Some species of dolphin have two stomachs, one for storage and one for digestion.

532.
Dolphins are born with a few hairs poking out of their chin, though these fall off pretty quickly.

533.
There are at least 44 species of dolphin in the world. Most live in the ocean, but there are also those that live in rivers, including the pink river dolphin that lives in the Amazon.

534.
Dolphins only ever have one set of teeth. Depending on the species, dolphins can either have very few or very many teeth. The long-beaked common dolphin can have up to 240 teeth, whereas Risso's dolphins have as few as 4.

535.
Dolphins sleep with one half of their brain at a time and keep one eye open. Scientists believe they do this to make sure they stick together, and to look out for predators.

536. Red Eyes

As a last resort in self-defense, the Texas horned star lizard can squirt a stream of blood directly from its eyes at any potential predators.

The lizard can spray up to a third of its total blood supply and it can travel several feet. The blood also contains chemicals that irritate any living creature unlucky enough to be in its path.

537. Mighty Beak

The hyacinth macaw has enough strength in its beak to crack open a coconut shell. It is also the largest of the macaws and measures 3.5 feet from beak to tail.

538. The Cave of Crystals

Buried 950 ft (290 m) below a mountain near the Mexican town Naica, Chihuahua, miners searching for ore deposits in 2000 were shocked to find a cave filled with giant crystals that measured 39 ft long (12 m) and over 3 ft wide (1 m).

539. Sounds Pink

Someone who has synesthesia (Greek translation "perceive together") is called a synesthete and can either smell words or hear colors. Some synesthetes might also hear music and see random shapes as a result. It is an incredibly rare condition that results from the merging of sensory and cognitive pathways.

540. Meganeura

300 million years ago, there existed a prehistoric dragonfly with wings that spanned over two feet. The Meganeura, as it is known, is the largest known flying insect to have ever existed on earth, and was big enough to hunt frogs and eat them with its mandibles.

541. Even though dragonflies have six legs, they cannot walk.

542. Learned Fear

Humans are born with only two innate fears: the fear of loud noises and the fear of falling. Every other fear, from spiders to water, is learned over time through life experience.

543. Language Barrier

Thanks to their vowel-filled language, Danish children can struggle to learn their mother tongue. At 15 months, Danish children speak 30% fewer words compared to Norwegian children, who are learning a similar language, and it takes nearly 2 years longer for Danish children to speak in the past tense. To better put it in to context, the Danish language has around 40 distinct vowel sounds, compared to English, which has about 14.

544. Red Nosed Liar

Scientists have discovered that when a person lies, the temperature around their nose increases. This is known as the "Pinocchio Effect."

545. Beard Economics

Late in the year 1698, Russian Tsar Peter I – also known as Peter the Great – implemented a tax on beards.

Peter had spent much time traveling through Europe with the goal of learning how European countries had become so successful. He traveled in disguise and even spent four months working at a shipyard for the Dutch East India Company. He later went to Great Britain, where he continued his study of shipbuilding, working at a Royal Navy dockyard, visiting factories, schools and even attending a session of Parliament.

Upon returning home, Peter wanted to reform Russia so that it could compete with its European neighbors. One of his reforms included the removal of all beards from all men across the country, and was seen as an attempt to replicate the "modern" Western Europeans he had met on his travels.

The policy proved incredibly unpopular, and eventually Peter realized he could make money for the state by imposing a beard tax. Nobles and wealthier individuals paid a much higher price than commoners, and each tax payer was given a token – silver for nobles and copper for commoners.

546. Occasionally, tired bees will fall asleep in flowers while collecting pollen.

547. BowieNet

The late great David Bowie launched his own internet service provider in the summer of 1998. Known as BowieNet, every user was given an email address ending in @davidbowie.com, had access to games, 5 MB of storage, and exclusive access to audio and video clips of the man himself.

548. Big Bat

The South Pacific is home to the largest bat species on Earth. The flying fox bat can weigh up to 2.6 lbs. (1.18 kg), and has a wingspan of up to 5 feet 6 inches (1.7 meters).

549. Is This a Dream?

You may have heard of déjà vu - the feeling you get when you feel like you have experienced an event before. But did you know that if you feel like you've experienced an event in a dream instead, it has a different name - déjà rêvé.

550. Angry Apes

Chimpanzees have been known to go to war with each other. In 1974, a group that was observed splintering apart spent the following four years attacking and ambushing each other for territory.

551. Pygg Pot

Although a lot of piggy banks take the form of pigs, the origins of the money saving pot had nothing to do with the animal. During the 15th century, a lot of household equipment was made from an affordable clay called "pygg." Whenever people at the time had an extra coin or two to spare, they would drop them in to a clay "pygg" pot.

Although the word pygg was originally pronounced "pug," the evolution of language over the years changed the sound of the word to "pig." English potters started shaping pygg pots in the shape of pigs as a play on words, and is why today the term piggy bank exists.

552. 300 Years of Entertainment

The memory capacity of the human brain far exceeds the average life expectancy of an individual – there is enough room in there to store 300 years of television.

553. 60s Hacker

The first computer password ever was stolen by a man named Allan Scherr in 1961. The password he stole was that of his colleague, Fernando Corbató, the inventor of computer passwords in 1960. Scherr stole the password because he wanted more time on the computer.

554. Clever Fish

Many people think that goldfish have very short memories, when in fact they have a memory span from three to five months. Not only that, but goldfish can recognize faces over time and can even be trained to do simple tricks.

555. The molds for manufacturing Lego are so accurate that only 18 out of every 1 million pieces are defective.

Thank you for buying and taking the time to read my first book, I hope you enjoyed it and perhaps even learned a few things! Writing, designing and publishing something like this takes an awful lot of time, and putting it out in front of an audience to be read and critiqued is a pretty scary experience.

To the brave pioneers who purchased my book when it had no reviews, you're the best! To those of you who have been kind enough to leave reviews, some with such positivity, I can't thank you enough.

If you have read my book and enjoyed it (or not), please consider leaving a review on Amazon. I see all of your comments and take them very much to heart, hoping to use all feedback to create and improve on my future books.

I wish you all the very best!

Printed in Great Britain
by Amazon

11687810R00086